# The Promise
# of
# HIS COMING

*A Panoramic View of the Biblical Doctrine
of the End of the World
and the Second Coming of
Jesus Christ*

## LESLIE H. WOODSON

**Institute for Biblical Excellence
Book Distribution Center
Elizabethtown, Kentucky**

# The Promise of His Coming

© 2001 by Leslie H. Woodson. All rights reserved.

Printed and packaged in the United States of America
by Cushing-Malloy, Inc., Ann Arbor, Michigan 48107

**Other Books by Les Woodson**

*A View from the Cornerstone*
*Divorce and the Gospel of Grace*
*Eight Days of Glory*
*Evangelism for Today's Church*
*Getting Ready to Live Forever*
*Hell and Salvation*
*How to Get to Heaven without Being Good*
*Make My Day!*
*Population, Pollution, and Prophecy*
*Signs in the Son*
*The Beginning*
*The Church: United or Untied*
*The Swinging Church*
*What You Believe and Why*

The book which you are preparing to read is a part of a widespread ministry devoted to the distribution of Christian reading materials used in the winning of the lost to Christ and the building up of the Church of our Lord. Should you desire to be a part of this endeavor, contact Les Woodson Ministries at 1-800-895-9729.

# Acknowledgments

This book would never have reached the publisher without the long and laborious hours of loving attention given it by the following friends:

Sylvia Dennison, whose professional expertise in mechanical preparation of layouts and design, deserves the highest of accolades.

Linda Jones, artist par excellence, has created, with striking effect, a cover which speaks to the theme of the book.

Jean Warf, proof-reader, whose trained eye has left no word un-scanned, has performed a yeoman's task.

Betty Woodson, a patient and supportive wife, whose tireless efforts in transferring words from the manuscript into the computer, is a wonder in herself.

# The
# PROMISE
## of
# HIS COMING

Les Woodson

# CONTENTS

Additional Thoughts on Prophecy
Concerns Often Overlooked
Symbolism in Numbers
Great Balls of Fire
Restoration Is Not Annihilation
What to Expect When Christians Leave This World

"In my Father's house are many mansions; if it were not so, I would have told you. And if I go to prepare a place for you, I will come again, and receive you unto myself; that where I am, there ye may be also.

"Knowing this first, that there shall come in the last days scoffers, walking after their own lusts, and saying, Where is the promise of his coming? For since the fathers fell asleep, all things continue as they were from the beginning of the creation.

"Cast not away, therefore, your confidence, which hath great recompense of reward. For ye have need of patience that, after ye have done the will of God, ye might receive the promise. For yet a little while, and he that shall come, will come, and will not tarry."

John 14:2-3, 2 Peter 3:3-4, Hebrews 10:35-37

# A PERSONAL NOTE FROM THE AUTHOR

The pilgrimage which has brought me to this point in my life has not been without sidetracks into dead end cul-de-sacs. As a very young Christian, converted at the age of thirteen and preaching by my fifteenth year, the second coming of Christ was a special concern for me from the outset. Barely in high school and with no formal training in biblical studies, my theological understanding was unrecognizable. I preached what I knew and I knew that my sins were forgiven, that Jesus was my friend, and that one day we would be together forever. Nothing more was needed to produce a fire in my bones so intense that the "boy preacher", as the public referred to me, was soon to become a spiritual arsonist. Everywhere the Lord sent me to tell the story, little fires were ignited in the hearts of others. The message was simple - repent, believe, and get ready to meet the Lord! What was lacking in theology was made up for in enthusiasm. And God blessed that beginning ministry with incredible results.

Prophecy was a total blank. The only prophecy proclaimed in those days was that Jesus is coming back to earth. Antichrist, translation, tribulation, millennium - these were words without meaning. Gradually, since my college years were spent in a secular university, my theological education developed with the Bible providing almost the only instruction available to me. And one cannot read the Word of God without confronting prophecy. The Bible is full of it. As would be expected, it was during this period that the new world of things to come started to open up.

Seminary opened many new vistas to me. Ideas were presented there which challenged nearly everything previously experienced and learned. Much of what was presented to us was more than helpful, but mixed with it was a sizeable portion of agnosticism relating to what the Bible had said to me. Biblical prophecy was one subject which was dealt a harsh blow. Any preacher who would be acceptable to the modern world just had to understand that these unenlightened ideas were antiquated. So, the tendency was to soften one's message in order not to be considered deficient in intellectual sophistication. While my preaching never neglected the second coming of Christ, it did suffer from a lesser emphasis on major prophetic themes.

God refused to let me ignore His Word. He had called me to preach and there would be no message unless it were His. It may be said that I was driven to a more intense study in order to clarify my mind where I had allowed the cobwebs of liberal theology to cloud the truth. And the result of that return to a literal interpretation of scripture was a clear and defining position on prophecy as developed in this book. In a way, my pilgrimage had come full circle, a return to the single truth given to a boy preacher, except that it was now grounded in a logical organization of the vast amount of factual information undreamed of at the beginning. John remembers hearing Jesus say, "My doctrine is not mine, but his that sent me. If any man will do his will, he shall know of the doctrine, whether it be of God, or whether I speak of myself" (John 7:16-17). It is safe to say that the general application of this truth is appropriate for every preacher within the Christian Church. My will is to know the truth and to present it regardless as to what some may think to the contrary. And this is so because I know full well that someday down the road I will have to give account of my stewardship.

Not every follower of Christ will agree with the promise and plan of God as we will watch it unfold in this book. There are several major views, which deal with biblical prophecy, and many minor variations on the major interpretations. Let none of us ever be bigoted enough to think he has a monopoly on truth. There is room for all at the foot of the cross and our salvation is not dependent on a right understanding of prophecy. Our salvation hinges on our saving faith in the death and resurrection of Jesus Christ. Each of us is responsible for being more than a shallow disciple whose mind is so open that it never closes on anything. It is not unusual for someone to reject outright the views on prophecy which I preach. And it is also not unusual, when such a person is asked for his view, to hear him admit that he has none. This is unacceptable for the Christian who wants to learn as much as possible about his faith. Together we walk with our risen Lord who encourages us to think seriously enough to be able to give a reason for the faith we share. So together we struggle for the truth which sets men free. It is to help with these struggles that this book has been written.

# SUGGESTIONS FOR SEEKING TRUTH

Recognize and admit first that none of us has 20/20 vision when it comes to finding the truth . . . Accept the fact that there is some truth in the worst of us and never all of it even in the best . . . By the same token, acknowledge that some false ideas are to be discovered in everyone, in the well-meaning as well as the misguided . . . Conceive truth as a life-long pursuit of sharing views with those who agree and those who disagree with one's fundamental assumptions . . . Never be afraid to hear an opposing side in any issue . . . Absolutely refuse to be arrogant and bigoted in the debate no matter how cherished a belief might be . . . Read everything available on the subject in spite of the suspicion that it may be heresy according to one's preconceived convictions. . . Truth can defend it's honor so do not fear for it's defeat by irreverent minds . . . When convinced of truth, hold firmly to it and espouse it without being shy, but do not be too proud to modify a position when new light is shed on it . . . Respect the claims of everyone, but weigh them by the teachings of Jesus who is truth incarnate . . . Never give up in the search because so many conflicting arguments persist . . . Be committed to the belief that truth can be discovered if only by degrees . . . Reject the cynical excuse that no one can ever know . . . Give priority to the teachings of the Bible on God's supreme revelation in Jesus Christ . . . Study the scriptures daily, taking advantage of every available opportunity to hear them presented . . . Pray for an open mind and receptive spirit in the presence of discussions of weighty subjects relating to God and men . . . Accept the obvious fact that the study of truth is a life-long pursuit and that when life is over here there will still be much to learn . . . And, above all, never forget that the communication of ideas with words is among the most difficult assignments in the world.

The inimitable Creek novelist, Nikos Kazantzakis, was struggling with this last suggestion when, at the outset of his classic book, SAINT FRANCIS, he wrote, "I had taken up my quill to begin writing many times before now, but I always abandoned it quickly: each time I was overcome with fear. Yes, may God forgive me, but the letters of the alphabet frighten me terribly. They are sly, shameless demons - and dangerous! You open the ink well, release them: they run off - and how will you ever get control of them again! They come to life, join, separate, ignore your commands, arrange themselves as they like on the paper - black, with tails and horns. You scream at them and implore them in vain: they do as they please. Prancing, pairing up shamelessly before you, they deceitfully expose what you did not wish to reveal, and they refuse to give voice to what is struggling, deep within your bowels, to come forth and speak to mankind."*

Verbal communication is a two way street. It is a give and take situation, an endeavor of reciprocal sensitivity. At points of detailed specifics, all of us must acknowledge built-in biases on the part of both the writer and the reader. No sermon, lecture, article, or book is the final answer on anything. Except the Bible, of course! If, after reading this book, the reader discovers an over-arching sense of revealed truth, the author will have done his work well.

*SAINT FRANCIS, Nikos Kazantzakis, Touchstone, Simon and Schuster, Inc., New York, 1962, p23.

# INTRODUCTION

The last half of the twentieth century was a period of apocalyptic fervor. The Second Coming of Christ and the end of the world was on everyone's mind. When the bomb was dropped on Japan in World War II, it was as if the human race were suddenly awakened to the very real possibility of the extinction of mankind. We began building bomb shelters in our basements and stacked them with supplies against such a catastrophe, never recognizing that such measures were no guarantee of survival and, much less, a solution to a world gone mad. Gradually, as the years passed, we grew accustomed to living with the bomb. A kind of numbness set in during the cold war when everyone knew that anything could happen and, if it did, we were all dead anyway. The end was not very far away.

Books began to appear from writers who related the world situation to prophecy. And this was a correct view to take. We were told that man had finally found a way to ignite the fuse which would culminate in the end of the world. The Bible talks about just such a conflagration at the Second Coming of Christ. Sermons were preached which attempted to explain what we should expect and when we should expect it. Some even gave us specific dates for the return of Christ in judgment. Everybody was being taught that the year A.D. 2,000 was a sacred year and that we should expect this event at about that time. Even scientists, without any thought of what the Bible says, were speculating that the turn of the millennium would be a year of awesome possibilities. It is not surprising that everybody became enamored with that date.

Christians should not be obsessed with a calendar of biblical events as much as with a seasonal schedule. Jesus, when warning

His disciples about the time of His coming, categorically stated, "You do not know the day or the hour" (Matthew 25:13 NIV). It would be reasonable to assume that this included the year as well! However, when the Twelve asked about the sign of His coming (Matthew 24), our Lord gave them very clear seasonal predictions. Often we hear someone insist that the world is getting worse and worse all the time (of course, some argue that it is getting better and better), but history does not run either consistently upward or downward. Surely no one would attempt to prove that conditions in the world today are morally worse than they were in the Dark Ages. History runs in cycles, each cycle having its highs and lows. The Bible tells us that it is when conditions on the earth are at one of history's degenerative lows that the Lord will come. This understanding of the Scriptures enables us to look for seasons instead of dates.

For persons looking for prophetic dates, we have passed "judgment day," and cynics are beginning to ask, "Where is this coming he promised? Ever since our fathers died, everything goes on as it has since the beginning of creation" (2 Peter 3:3 NIV). Could it not be that those of us who have been obsessed with dates are responsible for the smirk on the faces of those who ask such a question? We are not nearly as smart as we think. Jesus explained to us that the signs of His return and the end of the world would be quite discernible, but He cautioned us not to be too specific about our humanly devised calendars. Everything is in readiness and the eastern sky could explode into the brilliance of the return of Jesus at any moment. Paul reminds us, "You know very well that the day of the Lord will come like a thief in the night" (1 Thessalonians 5:2). It behooves us to be ready all the time, not to just get ready for a certain day.

The Bible is God's answer book. Within its contents is found the key to the past, present, and future. It is not the will of our heavenly Father to keep His children in the dark. Those who dwell in the dark have never experienced the divine light which dispels the fear that grows out of mystical literature. The Bible is the Word *revealed*, by the inspiration of the Holy Spirit, to men chosen by God to serve as channels for divine communication. It is the will of God that we know His plan of the ages, its stages of progression, and its consummation. Naturally, we cannot know that plan if we do not study it. It is the careful study of the Lord's design for the solution of the world's ills that we are attempting to pursue in these pages. Our prayer is that the Holy Spirit, who guides us into all truth, will enlighten our minds and warm our hearts as we see the eternal plan unfold in the word of prophecy.

The reader will be aware at once that there is no intention by the author to engage in fringe areas of religious fantasy. In the addendum at the end of the book, there are suggestions from secular history relating to the season of the end, but no certainties can be derived from these interesting predictions. One of the embarrassing admissions, which must be reckoned with, is the wide-spread dogmatism of some apocalyptic teachers for which there is no scriptural warrant. While the author is on solid ground in his own views on biblical prophecy, there is always enormous room for discussion and debate. No one has the final answer about specifics. What this book is concerned with is a thoughtful study of an indispensable and often neglected segment of the written Word of God. As the pages are read, let us make no rash judgments but, after much prayer and careful consideration, come to our own conclusions. It would be a coveted experience to hear from sincere readers who might further enlighten the author on this exciting discipline in prophecy.

Leslie H. Woodson

# Chapter 1

# The Burgeoning Family of Man

*Obeying a Mandate of the Creator*

At the dawn of human creation, God ordered Adam and Eve to "multiply and replenish the earth" (Genesis 1:28). This was the Creator's way of insuring the continuance of what He had begun, a kind of built-in perpetual momentum for human existence. Man was to be repetitive on his own. It was to be a chain reaction by which, once started on the earth, the human species would be permanently and perennially renewed. We are still engaged in the fulfilment of this divine mandate.

Only once did God interrupt the natural mushrooming process of human life. That was when the world became so corrupt that the earth had to be cleansed by a flood of waters which destroyed all but eight persons. When the waters subsided and Noah came forth from the ark into a world emptied of human life, God again repeated the order which He had given to Adam: ". . . Be fruitful, multiply, and replenish the earth" (Genesis 9:1). The plan had not changed since the beginning . God's will was that man, created in the divine likeness, should reproduce in kind until the whole earth was seeded with human life.

No one knows how old the earth is or precisely how long ago man appeared on the scene. Abraham lived about four thousand years ago at a time when the world seems to have been rather sparsely settled. Less than fifty million people may have inhabited the entire earth in his day. Since the period from

Adam to Abraham is not known to us, we have no way of determining what the rate of growth may have been on a time schedule.

In the days of Christ, there were approximately two hundred million people in the world. By the time of the seventeenth-century Puritans, the population figure had climbed to a half-billion. Within the next two centuries, the world's human family increased to one billion for the first time in history. Today there are over six billion people inhabiting the earth and scientists predict more to come. Any projection of population growth is dependent, of course, on many variables which cannot be known with any degree of accuracy. Estimates must be based on low, median, and high variants as well as constant fertility and no migration expectations.

It is easy to see that the rate of reproduction has accelerated with the passing millennia. The span of time required for the population to double itself has grown shorter and shorter. While the total doubled only once during the period from Alexander the Great to the great Mohammed (approximately one thousand years), today's population doubles twice in an average man's lifetime. If this rate of increase continues, it will not be long until there is standing room only on the earth.

Of all the divine commands given to man (many of which he has broken and refused to obey), the order to "multiply and replenish the earth" has been carried out to perfection. The fact of the matter is that we have *overdone* it! This is not to imply that God has been caught off guard by the excess numbers of people now in existence or the frightening prospects of further population growth. The Creator must have known that our present state of affairs would finally develop. And it is the opinion of this book that He has planned for just such an emergency.

*A General Projection*

An old, oft-used, and unbelievable trick is to ask a fresh recruit in the world of riddles which he would prefer – to work for a month at one hundred dollars per day or to work the same number of days at a penny for the first day, twice a penny the second day, and double the sum each day thereafter. Invariably, the would-be-laborer will impulsively choose one hundred dollars per day. It takes only a fleeting second to ring up a mental total of three thousand dollars for the month. That is a lot of money in anyone's calculation.

To ascertain the wages for thirty days, at a penny doubled each day, is considerably more difficult. At once, however, it is assumed that the total would be far less than three thousand dollars. When the facts are in, this assumption is proved incorrect. Working by this plan, thirty days labor pays $5,368,709.12. And if the month has thirty-one days in it, this figure becomes over ten million dollars!

By this simple arithmetic, one can readily see how the world's population has exploded so suddenly in our time. But then, as has been pointed out, there are variables which make such calculations much less simple. One must acknowledge that, at the beginning of the twenty-first century, women across the world are giving birth to fewer children than did their mothers. Some scientists are projecting that world population is slowly moving toward stabilization, possibly as early as 2050 A.D. Among demographers there are those who agree, speculating that the number of human beings on the earth may begin to drop by the middle of the twenty-first century. However, their more sober prediction is that, in the event of such a drop, it will not occur for at least 200 years. Frankly, little reason exists for becoming too upset about what may happen a century or two from now. For the present, the population increase is far from over. Every twelve months, nearly eighty million babies are born. That means that we are adding to the world's family the equivalent of a city the size of San Francisco every 72 hours. Our problems are growing.

## A Careful Diagnosis

In addition to the natural effects of doubling the population in shorter intervals, medical science has done a phenomenal job in conquering disease. Most of the scourges, which once took the lives of multitudes, have been attacked and defeated. Technologists have produced a maze of medical equipment which diagnose and treat both physical and mental maladies. There is nothing unusual about an ingeniously invented device absolutely taking over completely when the human body stops functioning. Iron lungs appeared on the scene a long time ago for the treatment of polio and now we have pacemakers which can be surgically placed within the body to force the heart to beat and to control its regularity. When kidneys cease to operate, the patient can be put on a machine which literally washes the poison from the blood and restores it clean to the body.

Little can happen to the modern man for which some corrective mechanical device is not readily available. This is true from the most minor illness to the major problems. More people are living longer because of the technological inventions of the scientific laboratories. Of late we are hearing more and more talk about freezing the human body under continued surveillance until a remedy is found for its disease. At that time, it is assumed that the body can be thawed and returned to new life. All this is still in the beginning stages, but in the light of the astounding things already happening, no one dares to suggest that such an eerie dream may not become a reality.

Miracle drugs are responsible for saving multiple thousands of lives each year — people who would have died in earlier times from the same ailments. The infant mortality rate has been greatly decreased and man's life span is being stretched out by new and better methods of treatment. A few scientists are even talking about physical immortality by which man may exist indefinitely by transplants. As parts of the body wear out or become defective, spare parts stored in a transplant bank can be surgically exchanged. This includes not only internal organs such as hearts, kidneys, livers, stomachs, and brains, but external faculties such as arms, legs, and reproductive organs as well. It is even suggested that eventually entire heads, not just the brain, will be transplanted. While one must react to such proposals for earthly immortality, it has to be admitted that the effort to achieve such a questionable boon might contribute to the projected population problems.

Cloning is now an ethical problem for both scientists and theologians. While it may have been achieved in the animal world, such a thing is clearly frightening in the human arena. Can we even imagine what would happen if men were allowed to play God in such matters? And who would those men and women be? The whole idea is unsettling to the sober mind. Hopefully, we will not add to our population puzzle by cloning more and more people.

With more people being born each year and the longevity of the human species being extended at the same time, it can be readily observed that our situation is bound to get worse. The human race is stretching itself at both ends rather than in the middle. Thus, in the foreseeable future, it is reasonable to assume that the numbers of children and youth (at one end of the age scale) and senior citizens (at the other end) will outdistance those of reproductive and middle years. Our generation gap is of no significance now in comparison to what it would be under conditions like those we have here projected for the future.

## A Possible Prognosis

All the knowledge of several branches of science is being combined to find a solution to the enormous problem of overpopulation. Few reputable scientists actually have much confidence that any of the proposed remedies will work. It is doubtful that enough people would cooperate with any suggested solution to make much difference. This is so for at least two reasons. Most of us do not fully grasp the gravity of the situation. We cannot really believe that possibilities could be as bad as we have heard. Furthermore, even those who have some understanding of the overall problem do not have consciences strong enough to encourage needed action. Most of us convince ourselves that what we ourselves do cannot make much difference since no one else is apt to do anything either.

The one approach thus far tried seriously is that of planned parenthood. Tons of literature have been written on the subject, government clinics have been established for instruction, churches and schools continue to contribute their influence, and free medical and mechanical aids are being provided for those too impoverished to pay for methods of control. Families are being urged to limit their children to two as a sensible way to slow down population growth. It is pointed out that, in many instances, children would be better cared for in smaller family units. This would be a fringe benefit in addition to stunting the population growth. Some married people have sought to fit into the new plan for smaller families, but the problem remains far from solved.

Contraceptives are now available in varied forms and almost anyone can get them regardless of age or circumstances. They can be worn, inserted, or taken orally. Surgery is often used to render a mother incapable of bearing children and men sometimes choose to undergo a minor surgery known as *vasectomy* which results in sterility. All of this is a part of our present approach to finding a practical and workable solution to the monstrous problem of too many people. Even if such solutions are advisable, it is not likely that the public at large will become concerned enough to buy into them.

*Questionable Experiments*

In addition to the fact that most people are paying little attention to the scare tactics of an alarmed scientific community, there are some disappointing developments in the whole plan. Easy access to contraceptives has encouraged untold millions of young people to engage in sexual intercourse who would have been afraid to do so without the modern security of the Pill. Unwanted and unexpected pregnancies have often resulted because of too much dependence on the promise of medical science.

As would be expected, the wide use of the Pill has carried with it a changed attitude on the sacredness of life. Abortion laws are being relaxed in the wake of a flood of so-called unplanned babies. Some estimates suggest that as many as a third of the babies born to first-time mothers are conceived outside the institution of marriage. This is a reflection on our changing views on the sacredness of human life. Though the birthrate has decreased slightly in general, the number of illegitimate births is on the increase. What we may be doing, in cutting down the size of families, is actually encouraging the birth of children to contraceptive-saturated single women. The whole institution of marriage may die and the race revert to existing and breeding like animals in the field.

With abortion available under the law for nearly any reason, we are now seeing clinics and doctors' offices filled with women standing in line to be miscarried. More and more the decision is being left to the mother – if she happens to have an understanding doctor. Even if this should eliminate a few hundred thousand babies a year, it will make no noticeable dent in the expanding population. And the emotional damage done to the mother – not to mention the growing disrespect for human life – might be far worse ultimately than permitting the fetus the right to live.

*Frenetic Remedies*

Debate has raged for years over whether a government, in order to control its population or balance its welfare budget, has the right to enforce a limit on the size of one's family. Under government welfare programs, unless carefully supervised, we have witnessed more and more children born to the indigent because the practice was financially profitable. As a result, our largest families have been found in the slums or among the extremely poor. An attempt is being made to correct this abuse.

To pass legislation which would limit these and other families, as to the number of children permitted, would require either a police state, such as exists in China, or a mass sterilization. Cutting down the welfare payment has helped, but such measures fail to get to the heart of the matter. One can imagine what it would be like to live in a police state where everyone is constantly checked to see whether new members have been secretly added to the family! The fear of living under that kind of brutality, which would possibly destroy either the new child or the parent responsible, is not hard to envision.

Enforced sterility seems to be a more humane method. Such a move may become a necessity in underdeveloped nations where starvation is a constant way of life. Certainly, it is better not to bring a child into the world than to give him birth without reasonable chance of survival. Yet, none of us can allow himself to think about this kind of procedure for very long without facing the grim possibility that some of the world's greatest men were born in extreme poverty. Under such a proposed plan, they would have been denied the right to be.

Aside from this haunting fact is the whole matter of ethics. Does a nation have the right to interfere in this most private and personal area of man's life? Are we engaged in a moral crime to treat people as though they were barnyard cattle emasculated at the will of others? Who would make the decision as to the size of families and what would be done with persons who managed to evade the law and "criminally" produced more children than permitted? And what would happen to mothers who were sterilized after having the allotted number of children in the tragic event the offspring died? The ethics involved in designing such a control measure cannot be overlooked.

## Out of This World

Oceanologists are talking not only of living off the nutrients available from cultivating the seas, but of living in the oceans themselves. If man could devise some inexpensive method of creating cities under water, he would help the immediate population squeeze. Unquestionably, scientists can do this for a few hundred men in a manned undersea station. But, to think of millions of people dwelling in similar circumstances is practically impossible from both sociological and economical perspectives. And if we should admit that miracles of science still happen, what will we do when the oceans are full?

That brings us to one of the most recent scientific proposals. Seriously projected as a possibility is the colonization of distant planets. Our worldwide space program placed astronauts on the moon to explore the possibility of man's living in its atmosphere. Billions of dollars have been invested in this exciting spectacular. Now it is known that men from the earth could not exist on the moon for two reasons: the lack of oxygen and the absence of water. Finding water on the moon could make it easier to establish colonies there or to build a fueling station for spacecraft. Water could be chemically split into oxygen and nitrogen, which could be used as a rocket fuel. Oxygen extracted from water could be used as a breathable atmosphere. The problem is that, in forcefully landing a mechanical device on the moon's surface, the splash we had hoped for was a disappointing cloud of dust! Furthermore, scientists are equally certain that the atmosphere on Mars and Venus is just as unacceptable to human life as we know it. Thus, the colonizing of these near planets is out of the question. Even if we could get enough people transported there to ease the pressure on earth, they could not survive without artificially controlled environment.

Perhaps there is a more distant planet or star where the environment would be more conducive to man's survival. Should we travel to the nearest star at the speed of light, the round trip would take nearly ten years. (The nearest star is 4.3 light years away. A light year is 5.88 million miles. Light travels at a speed of 186,000 miles per second. The round trip would be 50,568,000,000,000 miles which, at uninterrupted travel, would take eight and one-half years.)

But consider what these voyages would entail. How big could we build such rocket ships? How many people would they carry? How much would they cost and how many of them would be needed to get ahead of the population explosion? The plan to colonize outer space with earth people may be a good idea, but it has no chance of working. Apparently, God intended for us to stay right here! To continue to dream of living somewhere other than on this planet is to dwell in a world of gossamer wings with Peter Pan.

## An Impasse For Humanity

In light of the emerging dilemma of having just too many people on the earth, what can be done? Are there any measures known to man which can offer some ray of hope? If everyone would cooperate with the proposal to plan smaller families, there might be a chance. We are completely unrealistic to think that everyone – or even the majority of the world's peoples – will cooperate with anything suggested either by the governments of the world or the churches in it. Neither political persuasion nor ecclesiastical ethics have much influence on a race of people trained in permissiveness and bent on self-rule. And without the full cooperation of the men and women who create the problem, there can be no known solution.

Multitudes poke their heads in the sand and refuse to see the clamoring masses on tomorrow's horizon. Many have decided that the whole thing is hopeless anyway, so what is the use of worrying about it? More rational people are deeply concerned – some are even frightened for their grandchildren who will have to live in an overcrowded and impossible world. They are unwilling to cop out and let humanity go down the drain.

Men and women come up with newer and better ideas every day which appear to hold some possible answers. So far these human ideas only add to the complex confusion. Man is unequal to the task of saving his world. An example of the dilemma may be seen in the tug between the human ethic and the human reason. While we have managed to greatly reduce the infant mortality rate, we have now decided in favor of abortions to solve the overpopulation problem, and the disaster of having unwanted children, by doing what nature did before we got so smart.

And while we have prolonged man's life to the point where some scientists are predicting that persons born today have a good chance of living to be one hundred and fifty years old – at the same time we are debating the right and wrong of euthanasia. Is it possible that we have interfered too much with nature's simple remedies for overpopulation?

Added to the confusion is the fact that – though man has always considered war to be ethically wrong – never in history has there been such a worldwide denouncement of military combat. If the masses ever rule out war (which has been one method of controlling population in the past), what will this mean for the future? Let no one consider this an endorsement of war anymore than we are endorsing an increased mortality for infants! We are only looking at facts as they now exist. It is not difficult to see that everything we do complicates the whole problem until man is at last beginning to admit that he is at a dead end and no further maneuvering will help. Even scientists are now talking freely about the inevitable end of the world, and that could happen by any one of several grim catastrophes.

There is no easy solution to the problem. After all these centuries of time, we seem to have made little progress in the areas where progress is most needed. How fortunate we are to have a God who knows what is taking place and, without our consent, knows how to fix it.

# Chapter 2

# An Ensuing Contamination

## A Portrait of Confusion

As the number of people increases, more and more of earth's natural resources are exhausted. These resources may finally be depleted entirely because man will use them faster than the earth can reproduce them. But there is more to it than this. As these resources are used, they are not actually destroyed. They change form and are dumped back on the earth, in the water, or in the air. This means that more people using more resources produce more pollutants.

Ecologists are crying out in despair against what man is doing to his environment. It is evident that the world and the atmosphere around it are being turned into a giant dump heap. At the rate we are going, the human race may someday be like loathsome vermin crawling in a dunghill. And only if we develop different lungs and kidneys will we be able to breathe the air and drink the water. Everything is becoming contaminated.

It can readily be seen that population and pollution are related one to the other. If we can reduce the expected population growth we will automatically reduce some of the pockets of pollution. On the other hand, unless something is done soon about pollutants, the entire human family may be obliterated. That is an awesome thought but it is nonetheless true. It is not a matter of deciding which needs to be worked on first since both threats are closely interrelated. Both must be confronted at the same time, and something must be done at once. Perhaps it is worse than that. From a purely selfish concern, there may be little time to lose.

There are those who will insist that these remarks are too pessimistic. It depends on what one is looking for. Others may feel that they are too optimistic in that they suggest a *chance* for survival. Prevention for pollution saturation is destined to be at the top of the list of priorities in the effort to survive at all. The dedicated work of every world citizen must be brought to play if the suicidal trend is ever to be reversed.

A word of caution is in order here. In the controversy which rages around the custodial responsibility of man, great care needs to be taken in determining what is too much and what is too little. Every issue has two sides and compromise is a rare commodity. There are some among us who insist that the human race consumes so much of the earth's productiveness that moderation is not enough. What is required is total abstinence. So these well-meaning people reject every scientific and technological advancement which uses more of the good earth. The more radical among them demand that we return to an agrarian life-style, get rid of the internal combustion engine, repudiate everything resembling technology, provide our own animal skins, and live in caves. Of course, the animal rights advocates are opposed to this!

On the other side of the ledger appear those who have no sense of responsibility for the care and maintenance of the earth, the air, or the water. Everything is here for man's consumption and no one should be expected to replace what he has used. So we foul up the atmosphere with our noxious fumes, poison the streams with our industrial wastes, and drag every ounce of energy from the earth. Such people are the most destructive of all our parasites. Somehow we must find a rational course of action which allows the human race to enjoy its stay here by becoming more sensitive to the beneficent earth, by recycling everything which can be re-used, by giving back more than we take out, and by leaving the world a better place than it was when we were invited to come and live here.

## Air Too Risky to Inhale

It is a reasonable assumption that – within a few years – men will be able to live only in cities covered by huge domes under which the air is regularly purified. In order to go outside, one would be forced to wear a mask equipped with capsuled oxygen. Such excursions into the outside world would be discouraged except in extreme necessity. The risk would be too great even with a mask since the air might be so polluted as to be irritating to the flesh itself. Such a scenario may be a bit extreme, but at least it forces us to think.

The smog over Los Angeles today is like pure oxygen compared to what can be expected during the century so recently entered. And it will not be confined to particular areas, but will encase the whole globe like a wet, oppressive blanket. Settling on the world like fallout from a nuclear explosion are enormous quantities of smoke, ash, sulphur, dust, and numerous chemically-destructive gases. This is already the case and it gets worse every year.

If nuclear activity is accelerated, we will have magnified amounts of pollutants. A step-up in nuclear-powered machinery is all but inevitable. Future cars may have nuclear engines, though the move at present seems to be in the direction of electric cars. Even electric cars, however, could be dependent on nuclear energizing. Such energy may be harnessed in the operation of huge factories for production of both heat and power. The radioactive pollutants given off by the use of this method would be devastating to plant life as well as the human animal and his cousins in the fields.

Respiratory ailments are on the rise. Emphysema is swiftly challenging other modern diseases for the number-one spot on the list of human killers. Lung cancer threatens more men and women every day. No longer is it enough to discontinue smoking as protection against lung cancer. Just breathing the industrial, commercial, chemical-laden air seems to be enough to adversely affect even nonsmokers.

Continued dumping of our wastes into the air will ultimately so clog the biosphere that the rays of the sun could heat the particles intensely enough to raise the earth's temperature. A few degrees difference could be disastrous. With increased heat, the ice at the polar caps would melt and raise the level of our concerns enough to flood much of the land area. And with the population figures growing, the last thing we can afford to lose is a single acre of tillable ground. All this is directly related: more people, more technology, more pollution.

## Not A Drop to Drink

Lately we have been bombarded by warnings related to water contamination. From small townships to metropolitan industrial centers, our streams, rivers, lakes, and oceans are being filled with noxious waste. Unless the contamination is curbed soon, every major source of water may become so polluted as to be useless. Even in towns without factories, the water often has a bad odor and taste because of the excessive amounts of chemical additives necessary to make it safe to drink. Obviously, the chemicals themselves are damaging our own body systems. Again we are "caught between a rock and a hard place".

The world's seas are filled with plant life called *phytoplankton* which produces and sustains about 65 percent of the oxygen in our atmosphere. Because of pollutants, this plant life is being destroyed in great quantities. Yet, we continue to dump human and industrial refuse into the oceans as man shuts his eyes to the death he is creating for himself and his children. The fact that fish in the seas are often so filled with chemical wastes that they are unfit to eat is a commentary on the plight we are describing.

Since the beginning of creation not one drop of water has been added to or subtracted from the original supply. It changes forms and is used over and over again, but eventually it returns to the seas where the cycle is repeated. Salt from gradually-rising water tables is now being found in underground fresh-water channels. If the ice caps should melt (as mentioned above), the salt from the seas would render much of the land untillable – land not covered by ocean water but still recipient of salt seepage.

*Where on Earth*

According to some experts, at least two acres of productive land are needed to provide the minimal diet requirements for one man's basic health needs. A comparison of the number of acres of tillable soil available with the number of people living in the world indicates that this ratio is too fluid to arrive at a precise figure. However, if the population increases at anything near the present rate of growth, the number of acres of productive soil available per person will be less and less.

As if this were not enough of a problem to haunt us, vast stretches of this usable soil are being carelessly neglected, desecrated, and covered with defiling refuse. Manifestly, our garbage has to be placed somewhere. If it is not dumped in the seas, then it has to be dumped on the earth. There is nowhere else to put it. Of course, it has been suggested that giant spaceships could transfer our garbage into the heavens beyond the pull of gravity. This would load space beyond our earth with even more particles to be heated by the sun and thus raise the world's temperature. Such earth fever would be disastrous for human life. A variation on this proposal: Garbage could be rocketed toward the sun where both the carrier and its rotting cargo would be incinerated. The cost of such a sanitation service in itself would be enough to discourage use of this plan.

We already have arrived at the point where it is not easy to find additional land area which is needed for burying the dead. Mausoleums provide one way of using less space. It has been suggested that bodies could be buried in stacks or interred upright. Cremation appears to be a good way to conserve land area, but a massive program of cremation would add more pollutants to the atmosphere! There is no simple answer. Maybe there is no answer at all.

Animal life and plant growth are both having a rough time in this maze. Pesticides and chemical treatment of plants have proved injurious to the animals that need the plants for food. In turn, people who eat these animals are also harmed. Artificial foods are being made to fill the gap created by this problem. Eventually we may have to face illnesses resulting from too much food manufactured with synthetic nutrients.

## The Legitimate Fear of Starvation

About four million men, women, and children die of starvation each year. That is a staggering figure. With famine conditions multiplying, the number grows even larger. To put it another way, over 400 people starve to death every hour. Or again, a family of seven people die from starvation every second. In America, we are hard pressed to grasp the horror of this fact because ours is a land of plenty where no one witnesses masses of starving people in the streets. Nevertheless, in many countries of the world, it is an almost impossible task to bury the bodies as fast as they fall. And no one in his right mind can doubt that such conditions may someday prevail right here in the land of Western luxury.

With our soil being depleted of its natural growth qualities and poisoned by our contaminants, it cannot be expected to produce enough for as many human beings as are anticipated within the next hundred years. As food becomes less plentiful, it will be priced higher until it is out of reach of all but a select group of wealthy citizens. Every inch of space in one's yard (and there will be no yards left if population continues to explode!) will be cultivated carefully to eke out a bare subsistence. Looking at these prospects makes the words of Jesus come alive: ". . . there will be famines . . . in various places: all this is but the beginning of the sufferings" (Matthew 24:7,8 RSV). The days of which He spoke are here and the sane man knows that they are bound to get worse.

The earth, in spite of our agricultural advances, may find it increasingly difficult to produce enough food for twelve to fifteen billion people. If we are seriously counting on cultivating the sea for foodstuff, we are not being very realistic. With the growing mortality rate of sea life there is little chance of much help there. Starvation is right in the middle of our radar screen and the human race is precisely on course.

Someone will immediately reply that such a deplorable situation will control the population explosion. To be sure, increased starvation will cut down the numbers of people in the world, but the human family will be "lucky" enough to utilize its technological skills so that the number of deaths will never equal the number of births. This will be done for a while by artificial foods even if they are nothing more than nutrient saturated energy pills. It may be that enforced dieting will become the order of the day. Food will be rationed under carefully supervised governmental control. And all this will finally result in a dictator for the whole world who will demand that his identifying mark be branded on every forehead before one can buy food at all (Revelation 13:17). Undoubtedly, some form of tranquilizer will also be administered to people to numb them to reality and curb hunger riots. Population and starvation are closely intertwined, but it is prophetically clear that the latter — terrible as it will become — will not *solve* anything.

## At Our Wits' End

Caught up in this melee of insurmountable obstacles to any kind of satisfying life in the future, man is apt to despair and lose hope. There is nothing man can do to solve the riddle of overpopulation. There is no *human* answer. Only those who are too obtuse to see what is happening, or those who are too obsessed with their own self-sufficiency, can possibly continue to trust any man or group of men to save the world. A few decades ago the old liberals were sure that – given enough culture and education – the world would get better and better. They have been proved wrong – dead wrong. With all the refinements of modern education and philosophy, the picture gets blacker. Man can provide no escape from the frightening prospects which lie ahead.

Let no one think that there is no way out of this alarming mess (as though it cannot be done unless man does it). Our whole problem stems from our neglect of God's will and disregard for His prophetic plan. The masses have never had time to read His Word and study it seriously. Perhaps it has not been so much a matter of lacking time as lacking the disposition to open oneself to divine truth. Whatever the reason may have been, there is appalling ignorance of the heart of the Bible and terrible fear for that very reason. There is an answer but it is not of man's making. It is God's answer and it is becoming clearer every day.

# Chapter 3

# The Coming Rapture

## The Countdown We Remember

Excitement is in the air. Men in white are scurrying about in a last-minute effort to get everything ready for blast-off. Specialists are poring over their intricate instruments, checking and rechecking every detail to be sure that nothing fails to function in the electronic devices so important to a space flight. Tracking stations have been set up all across the world to check the trajectory of the rocket-powered module. Mechanics specially trained for the job are busily engaged in fueling operations and last minute adjustments. A lazy vapor seeps from the side of the mighty rocket, squatting on its base like a wild beast, ready to attack without warning.

Three men, outfitted in luminous, balloonlike suits reminiscent of a Buck Rogers movie, take an elevator to the capsule. Over their heads are glass bubbles which make them look like imaginary creatures from another planet. They look peculiar and walk in a strange kind of mechanical manner. These men have been training for months – perhaps years – for this moment. The discipline through which they have put themselves is incredible. And they have committed themselves to an austere way of living because they believe in what is going to happen. They are a part of a plan which is much bigger than any of them as individuals. No doubts linger in their minds. Though no one has ever been to the moon before, there is not the slightest lack of confidence that it is going to take place.

Masses of people are skeptical. Talk of going to the moon has been heard here and there for years. Some actually think it is about to transpire – but not everyone. Three strange-acting men will probably be killed in some kind of fiery blast before it is over. The whole idea is so idiotic. Why can men not stay here on earth where they belong? Why does anyone want to go flying off into some unknown world only to get blown up? It will never happen. Yet, the silly countdown continues: "T minus twenty-two minutes and counting . . . ." It would be a laughing matter if it were not that somebody is going to be killed in the wreckage. The whole scheme will make the United States the laughingstock of the whole world. Mumbling and shaking their heads at the stupidity being seen portrayed on their television screen, they retire to the kitchen for a snack. It is all so ridiculous.

"T minus three minutes and four seconds and counting . . . ." They rush back to the screen still shaking their heads in unbelief. "Four – three – two – one – ignition!" An explosion of orange fire rolls from beneath the rocket and slowly the big bird begins to rise from its nest. In a matter of seconds it is picking up speed and in only a few more it is out of sight. Technicians report all systems are working and the rocket is on course. Within a few minutes it is reported that the ship has passed the first danger point. Soon the first stage is completed on time, second stage on target, and the mission looks like a success. A few days later the astronauts are on the moon. Believe it or not, it had happened. What had been predicted was now history and those who did not believe could not accept what had taken place. Some even insisted that the whole thing was a pre-planned hoax, photographs and all. But that's the way it was.

## The Countdown We Anticipate

Excitement is in the air. But it is not at Cape Canaveral. It is all over the world. There is an air of expectancy shared by

multiple thousands of Christian believers.  To be sure, not
everyone is excited.  Many are so caught up with the awesome
problems of a crumbling launching pad that they have forgotten
or ignored the possibility of a launch altogether.  For a long time
this day has been planned.  Men and women, young people and
children, in invisible white garments, are scurrying about to be
sure that everything is ready.  Specialists in prophecy are
checking every detail and the trajectory is being studied carefully.
Numbers of workers are set to the task of fueling and making
adjustments through prayer and witnessing.

The difference between this launch and the one at the Cape is
that  everybody involved in the preparation is going – not just
three astronauts.  Those engaged in getting themselves ready
and recruiting others for the journey into space are thought to be
a little odd.  They have a stance which reminds one of the
strange look and walk of the balloon-suited men in the moon
capsule.  But these people are a part of a plan, a *divine* plan,
which they are as certain will be completed as were those
dedicated astronauts confident of their flight to the moon.

There has been talk occasionally across the years about this
religious notion of a flight into the heavens with Christ, but not
many have paid any attention to it.  It all seemed a little frenetic
to say the least.  It is true that some people were preparing 'way
back in the first century, but it did not happen.  The countdown
has been going on for two thousand years.  Some think that
there have been times when God has interrupted the countdown
with "T minus thirteen hundred years and holding . . . ." or "T
minus four hundred fifty years and holding . . . ," but most
Christians believe that the counting has continued since the
Ascension of Christ.  The prophetic  timetable of God remains
unaltered.

For two thousand years men and women have been training,
disciplining themselves while the masses laughed them to scorn.
To the man of the world – whether he is in the organized church
makes little difference – the preparation which persons in the true

Church are making for lift-off is a laughing matter. He will not even listen to what is being said. He is a non-Bible bigot who refuses to hear anything which he has decided is unacceptable to a sophisticated being on the pure basis of human logic alone. And so the world goes about its reckless way, disregarding all the signs that point to blast-off time. Yet, the countdown continues and the voice of Deity Control is saying, "T minus thirty years and counting ... T minus twenty years and counting ... T minus fifteen years and counting ...." No one knows for sure when the last seconds will tick away: "Four – three – two – one – ignition!"

## The World As a Giant Launching Pad

In the moon shot, and all later launches, a predetermined location on the earth's surface was chosen for launch. Only from one spot could the astronauts be catapulted into their orbit around the moon. The chosen place was a restricted area at the edge of the Atlantic Ocean. Persons outside the grounds of Cape Canaveral were able to share in the historical lift-off only by watching from afar. Even men who were closely associated with the lunar program and actually on the grounds were not permitted to ride in the nose of the rocket. Three men out of all the world's billions were to experience the mighty surge of power which sent one lone spacecraft into the starry heavens.

The launch, which is scheduled to soon take place is not set for some restricted place on the earth's surface. When the lift-off comes, it will happen all over the earth at one and the same time. Neither space nor time constitutes a serious problem for Him who created both. The Eternal Spirit is always present in every place. And when He decides to overrule the forces of gravity which keep man on the earth, even graves will be broken apart and emptied of their tenants. So irresistible is the drawing power of the Lord that men and women of like nature, both dead and alive, will be magnetically pulled to Him. Millions of people from all over the world, people who have committed their lives in faith to the redeeming Christ, will join the One who saved them in the clouds of heaven.   Nowhere in the Scriptures is this more vividly described than in the letter of Paul written to the Thessalonians.

> For this we declare to you by the word of the Lord, that we who are alive, who are left until the coming of the Lord, shall not precede those who have fallen asleep. For the Lord himself will descend from heaven with a cry of command, with the archangel's call, and with the sound of the trumpet of God.   And the dead in Christ will rise first; then we which are alive, who are left, shall be caught up together with them in the clouds to meet the Lord in the air; and so we shall always be with the Lord.
>
> 1 Thessalonians 4:15-17 RSV

When the Savior was here in the flesh, He employed this divine drawing power in a most unique manner on one particular occasion.  It was a kind of prelude to that final day when He will "descend from heaven with a cry of command."  Arriving at the home of Mary and Martha, after their brother had been dead for four days, Jesus had the stone removed from the opening of the tomb.  Then, with a loud "cry of command," He called the name of him who was interred there and ordered that he come forth. At once the man arose, was stripped of his grave clothing, and enjoyed the fellowship of his Lord (John 11:1-44).  Someday *every* grave which shelters the body of Christ's disciple will break open at that "cry of command."   Had Jesus not called Lazarus by name that day in Bethany, the entire cemetery would have been emptied!  And when He comes with that divine shout from the clouds, every redeemed man, woman, boy, and girl will hear his name in that cry and will rise to meet the Lord.

There will be apostles whose bodies have lain in some

unknown grave since the first century, unsung heroes of the faith spanning two millennia, and martyrs from many lands in that great crowd of the redeemed. Not one will be forgotten by God. Black Christians from the heart of Africa will be there. Brown-skinned followers of the Christ will join them from India, Spain, Mexico, and South America. Europeans, Orientals, Asians, Scandinavians, Polynesians, Australians, North Americans, and islanders from all over the earth will converge at that meeting in the air. The aged will be there and the children. Every period in Christian history is to be represented. From every quarter of the earth, the people of the Lord shall come pouring in to be together forever. At last the Church for which He prayed will be one (John 17:23).

### Multitudes Will Escape Death

Since the beginning of time, all men have shared the lot common to humanity. With the exception of Enoch and Elijah, every man born from Adam until the present time has been destined to die. It is true that those who die in the Lord will rise again when Christ returns. This is what Jesus was talking about when He said to Martha, "I am the resurrection and the life; he who believes in me, though he die, yet shall he live, and whoever lives and believes in me shall never die" (John 11:25,26 RSV). In this word about never dying, the Lord has reference to spiritual death which has no power over the Christian believer. But there are some people who will have the distinct privilege of never dying at all — spiritually or physically. These are the redeemed of the Lord who are still alive at the coming of Jesus the second time.

Being as human as the rest of us, in his desire to meet the Savior without the need of physical death, the Apostle Paul hoped that the Lord would come again in his own lifetime. In fact, he felt strongly about such a possibility. And that is the only correct attitude for Christians in every age. In his anxiousness for the *parousia* (the Greek New Testament word for the Second Coming which we will use in this book), Paul excitedly explained to the members of the little church in Corinth:

> Lo! I tell you a mystery. We shall not all sleep, but we shall all be changed, in a moment, in the twinkling of an eye, at the last trump. For the trumpet will sound, and the dead will be raised imperishable, and we shall be changed.
>
> 1 Corinthians 15:51,52 RSV

The *trumpet sound,* to which he refers, is the same as that mentioned in the earlier reference from the epistle to the Thessalonians. The "cry of command" and the " sound of the trumpet of God" will usher in "the resurrection of the just" (Luke 14:13). But it will also be the divine signal for a glorious change in those who are alive when the sound is heard. The apostle calls this change "a mystery." We cannot imagine how God will effect this metamorphosis, but there is no question about the certainty of its happening. It will happen "in a moment, in the twinkling of an eye." What God will do for His people at that time will be sudden and complete. There is no hint of an evolutionary change. The transformation will be as instantaneous as the change which comes to a hard grain of corn held over the fire until it pops into a fresh, white form.

No other explanation is given about the kind of change we may anticipate than Paul's statement about that which is perishable becoming imperishable and that which is mortal becoming immortal (1 Corinthians 15:42-44,53). Apparently the transformation depicted here is the same as that hinted by John when he writes: "We are God's children now; it does not yet appear what we shall be, but we know that when he appears we shall be like him for we shall see him as he is" (1 John 3:2 RSV). The change which materializes, in that split moment of time, will completely prepare the living believers for life in a brand-new dimension of existence. Whatever needs altering will be altered and made new even as will be the resurrected bodies of the dead believers. "Our citizenship is in heaven. And we eagerly await a Savior from there, the Lord Jesus Christ, who, by the power that enables him to bring everything under his control, will transform our lowly bodies so that they will be like his glorious body" (Philippians 3:20,21 NIV).

When Jesus predicts those things to be looked for immediately prior to the Second Advent of the Son of God, He emphatically affirms the divine Word with an amen: "This generation shall not pass away, till all be fulfilled" (Luke 21:32). What generation was the Lord talking about? Without doubt, He was talking about the generation of people who see these awesome signs of the end time, especially the troubles met by the rebuilt state of Israel. The people, who see the prophecies related to the days immediately before the appearance of the Lord from heaven, will be those who will be alive to be caught up into the clouds of His coming.

## Christ's Coming in the Air

For much too long a time, well-meaning Christians have argued strongly that the Second Coming of Christ is to be understood in a figurative, spiritualized way. To speak of the parousia as an event yet to take place at a precise point in time, when the whole world must reckon with a returned Christ, is a thought repugnant to some. In an ingenious attempt to get around the biblical prophecy regarding the return of Christ as King, the Christian community has created several fanciful interpretations.

Persons who do not know the Scriptures well are often heard to say  that the Second Coming of Jesus has already taken place. The Lord returned on the day of Pentecost in the person of the Holy Spirit. Clearly the New Testament teaches that the Holy Spirit, who is the present tense of Christ, must still be distinguished in some way from the One who is yet to come again. Shortly before His death, our Lord spoke of the Spirit who would come at Pentecost as the One "who proceeds from the Father" and promised that He would "bear witness to me [Christ]" (John 15:26 RSV). Just prior to this word is another in which Jesus calls the Holy Spirit "another Counselor" (14:16 RSV). What we have here is an identification for both the Lord Jesus and the Holy Spirit. While the Spirit is the present tense of Jesus, He is "another" in the sense that the bodily presence is not now with us, but will be following the Second Advent. Furthermore, all the New Testament was written after the day of Pentecost and yet, it invariably speaks of the *parousia* as a future event. Not a single New Testament writer so much as hints that the Second Coming was over and consigned to some past moment in history.

Conveniently, a neat little explanation has been put forward by those who would relegate the doctrine of the Second Advent to the time of the believer's death. This would mean that the event is repetitious and contingent upon man's experience. Nowhere does the Bible say that Christ comes to us at death. To be sure, He assured His disciple that He would be with them "even to the end of the world" (Matthew 28:20), but this was a promise of continued support for the believer which has nothing to do with a special divine coming at death. We would be more in line with the general tenor of the Christian revelation if death were conceived of as a *going to* Christ rather than a *coming of* Christ to man. All of us are accustomed to hearing the fourteenth chapter of John used at funerals. While it is not wrong to read these words under such circumstances, the Messianic promise, "I will come again and receive you unto myself" (John 14:3) is not fulfilled. It will happen at the *parousia*.

As if this were not enough, some have also insisted that Jesus comes every time we meet to worship. "Where two or three are gathered together in my name, there am I in the midst of them" (Matthew 18:20). There is no mention here, however, about an actual *coming*. On the contrary, it is the same truth which has been observed above in relation to the *continuous* presence of the Lord in an undergirding way. The daily consciousness of His presence with us must not be mistaken for the unique *appearance* of Christ in the clouds.

Emphatically, the Bible speaks again and again of a visible bodily return of Jesus Christ to the earth. Every one of the prophecies in the Old Testament about His First Coming, the birth of Jesus in Bethlehem, was literally fulfilled. Most of the promises in both the Old and New Testament which point to His Second Coming have come to pass already. Incidentally, there are hundreds of these prophetic promises throughout the Bible. And there is no reason to assume anything other than that every prophecy of the return of our Lord will be as *literally* fulfilled as were those which predicted His birth.

As the disciples stood on the Mount of Olives anxiously watching the Ascension of Jesus, an angelic messenger assured them: "This same Jesus, which is taken up from you into heaven, shall so come in like manner as ye have seen him go into heaven" (Acts 1:11). The disciples saw their Lord ascend. He was a bodily form which rose from the earth and vanished from human sight. But He is not gone forever. One day we will see Him come again "in the same way" as those early followers watched Him depart. And when He comes every Christian believer will be caught up into the clouds to meet Him and join the resurrected dead who instantly precede them.

## Earlier Rapturous Experiences

Genesis tells the story of the translation of Enoch (Genesis 5:21-24) and a similar incident in the life of Elijah is recorded in 2 Kings 2:9-12. In the letter to the Hebrew Christians, we find a reference to the first of these two godly men of old.

By faith Enoch was taken from this life, so that he did not

experience death; he could not be found, because God
had taken him away. For before he was taken, he was
commended as one who pleased God.

Hebrews 11:5 NIV

Let us look for a moment at this lone, holy man who lived in
a time of incomparable wickedness before the Great Flood.
Succinctly, his story is told in the book of beginnings: "All the
days of Enoch were three hundred and sixty-five years. Enoch
walked with God; and he was not; for God took him" (Genesis
5:23,24). According to the Mosaic account, this man served God
faithfully and was rewarded by being translated (removed or
transferred from this earth to the heavenly sphere with the Lord).
He was *caught up* and thus escaped the awful Flood which was
soon to come upon the ancient world as judgment on its
exceeding wickedness and corruption. For reasons unknown to
us, God rewarded Elijah for his faithful prophecy in the same
way. Perhaps it was because Elijah must appear as one of the
two witnesses in the coming tribulation (Revelation 11:4-12; cf.
Malachi 4:5 and Matthew 17:3). The two witnesses (the other of
which is probably Moses whose death is shrouded in mystery)
will be killed during that awful time. No man should have to die
twice!

Both Enoch and Elijah were early types of the translation of the
Church which must soon come to pass. But we must not
overlook Noah whose times are compared by Jesus to the days
of the coming of the Lord (Matthew 24:36-39). Before the Flood,
while the men and women around him continued in their
corruption and made fun of anyone who believed in a coming
deluge of water, Noah remained faithful. He was obedient to
God in building the ark even though everybody was sure that he
was wrong. Refusing to have any part in the godless and
debauched practices of his pagan neighbors, the fearless servant
of the Lord warned everyone whom he saw to repent and enter
the ark. The evil was so entrenched, however, that there were no

converts save his own family.

When the rains began to fall and the underground water systems overflowed their bounds, Noah and the seven members of his family entered the boat which God had told him to build. Judgment fell in death upon the peoples who had laughed without repentance, the multitudes who had jeered as they listened to this honest man's preaching. But Noah and his family were *caught up* above the terrible judgment meted out to a world of unbelief. Safely housed in their boat with the Lord, they outrode the storm of God's wrath. Jehovah had lifted up His own and spared them the fearful hour of tragedy.

Enoch, Elijah, and Noah are all archetypes of the coming lift-off of the people of God. Another man named Methuselah is also a rather interesting type at whom we will look later. In each of these men can be seen similarities to that grand and glorious event which is so rapidly moving toward launch date. It may be that God has given us examples like Enoch to show how it can happen – how suddenly and permanently. If it happened to one man, then it can happen to millions of men today. And if this thought alarms and frightens us, it is likely that we do not share the joyous hope of the early Christians. It was at the conclusion of Paul's vivid description of what we have been talking about in this chapter that he said, "Comfort one another with these words" (1 Thessalonians 4:18).

## A Revised Census Needed

By now it will have become obvious to us that this book is more about prophecy than it is about either earth's bulging number of people or its growing contamination. This does not alter the fact that overpopulation and its related problems are all bound up in the total plan of God. At the very time when overcrowded conditions on the earth are becoming intolerable, the Lord will thin out the masses in His own way. There will be a relieving of the situation for the world by the exit of millions of the Lord's people. The problems on the earth will afterwards become increasingly worse, but at least there will be temporary respite to the population problem. If the removal of the Church did nothing else for the unbelievers left behind, it should convince them that God does have solutions to inescapable riddles which human ingenuity cannot handle.

All through the New Testament we are led to believe that Christians are a minority group. In every generation, the Christian community has been less than half the world's population (except when the Emperor Constantine made it the state religion). When it is admitted that the larger percentage of churchmen are only nominal Christians, it begins to look like the prediction of Jesus was *literally* true: "For the gate is narrow and the way is hard, that leads to life, and those who find it are few" (Matthew 7:14 RSV). Yet, John sees a great multitude which no man can number (Revelation 7:9) in the coming Kingdom. There is no contradiction here at all. In every generation, the redeemed are in the minority, but when those of all the centuries are brought together at the end of the age, the throng will be numberless except to God who numbers even the hairs on our heads (Luke 12:7).

Though believers living at the time of our Lord's coming may be far smaller in number than the apostate church is ready to admit, there will be a sizeable number of persons suddenly evacuated. If the Savior should come today and only ten percent of the world's population were ready to meet Him, the crowd would still be over 600,000,000! That would make a noticeable difference in the people bulge.

Not only would such a *lifting* out of the people of the Lord reduce the living population, but it would also ease the problem of having inadequate burial grounds. Great numbers of graves would be abandoned and left vacant for new tenants. The redeemed of two thousand years would take leave of their cramped burial chambers for the meeting in the air. Can anyone begin to conceive of how many would be included in history's greatest grave robbery?  No wonder the throngs seen by John were like the stars in number!

## A Guide to Survival

Thinning the world's population creates a little breathing room, but not for long.  In the seven years to follow, the full force of satanic wrath will be unleashed upon the remaining citizens of the world.  The only way to survive is to be prepared when the Lord comes.  Did not Jesus insist on the importance of such preparedness when He said, "Be ready; for the Son of Man is coming at an hour when you do not expect" (Matthew 24:44 RSV).  None can miss the point of the parable of the ten virgins. It is an admonition not to be foolishly unprepared when the bridegroom [Christ] comes, but to "Watch . . . for you know neither the day nor the hour" (25:13 RSV).  One of two things must happen to every person when the Lord returns – either he enters into the joy and festivity of the marriage of the Lamb or he is left forever outside.

Writing to the believers in Thessalonica, Paul warns of the sudden and unannounced appearing of Jesus "like a thief in the night" and insists that Christians "are not in darkness" so that day should surprise them (1 Thessalonians 5:2,4).  Another way of putting it is to insist that true believers will not be caught off guard because they walk in the light of the Spirit and expect the parousia at any moment.  And to state it in reverse manner, to argue against His return or to ignore its imminence is to reveal that one is in the darkness and unprepared for the event toward which all history moves.

In following sections of this book, we shall look at what those, who are left on the earth after the evacuation of the Church has taken place, will have to face.  It will be seen that existence on this planet, after the Church is gone, will be all but impossible. Of course, some form of the apostate church will still be in operation with its ecclesiastical hierarchy in league with the enemies of God. The way to survive is to be *ready* for the coming in the clouds and the reunion of the children of God in blessed and glorious deliverance. The King is coming and His reward for the redeemed in Christ will be the fulfilment of the divine plan for those whom He knows and loves. No one need miss it. But the Kingdom is a certainty only for those who are prepared.

We cannot be reminded too often that every believer must sharpen his focus on the imminent return of Jesus Christ. Only one proper attitude should characterize the Christian disciple ... he expects the *parousia* every day at any hour. That is the only way to be prepared for the meeting in the air.

It is such an easy thing to sit back, relax in our supposed security, and assume that everything will take care of itself. But, of course, it will not. Unless we do something about our broken relationship with God, there is no ray of sunshine on the horizon. But, on the other hand, those of us who get our hearts right with the Lord are assured that the future is bright, not with hope, but with certainty.

# Chapter 4

# A Reason for Divine Evacuation

## The Church As a Special People

To understand the origin, mission, and destiny of the Christian Church, one must go all the way back to the beginning of time. Unless the divine panorama of biblical history is seen in its entirety, there is no conceivable way to properly grasp the meaning of the Church. Without seeing the locus of the *ecclesia* (Greek New Testament word for *church* meaning the "called out") in its total historical context, we are like men looking at only a fragmentation of the divine picture. Since this is so manifest as to require no further insistence, let us take a moment to trace the acts of God in developing His plan from Eden to Pentecost.

One created being was already on the earth before the appearance of man. In the Old Testament he is called *Lucifer* (Isaiah 14:12-15). He had been originally created by God as the head of the angelic beings who served before the Lord. The prophet describes him as "the anointed cherub that covereth" (Ezekiel 28:14) which probably has to do with his angelic headship and general surveillance of the newly-made world. Being given this exalted position of authority, which made him second only to God Himself, was too much even for an angel. Thus we encounter the origin of evil in the rebellion of Lucifer and his resultant expulsion from the heavenly abode of God. This accounts for Satan's (the New Testament name for Lucifer) presence in the Garden of Eden and his subtle tactics used to interfere with the Creator's plan.

Adam and Eve were created without sin and placed in a new world of innocent purity. In a sense, man was the divine replacement of Lucifer in a different dimension of existence. Adam was to be God's chosen servant, even closer to Him than the angels, and was to be given dominion over the whole earth (Genesis 1:26). Everything was to be under his surveillance and authority including all other living creatures as well as the actual land itself. But Satan seduced the woman, who in turn seduced the man, to do things his way rather than God's. In the human surrender to the tempter, the scepter of dominion was wrested from man and controlled by Lucifer. Thus Satan assumed the role of "god of this world" (2 Corinthians 4:4) and man's long struggle began – a battle which continues to this day.

As would be expected, the ancient world grew exceedingly wicked as it followed the leading of man's chosen god. No one was in a position to be a mediator between the world's people and the world's Creator because sin had rendered the entire race incapable of access to God. The result was that the situation grew worse until the world was "corrupt and over-run with violence" (Genesis 6:11 RSV). Ultimately, the plight of man became so desperate, and the plan of God so completely perverted, that the Flood of divine judgment wiped the surface of the world clean of human life. Only one family was left to make a fresh start.

After the Flood had subsided, God renewed the original dominion of man for Noah (Genesis 9:2). This one man, out of all who lived, could be trusted to carry out the divine design. Once more the Lord would seek to rule the human race through Noah and specially chosen descendants. But, alas, as men began to multiply again, they forgot God and, under the subtle strategy of the "god of this world," decided to construct a universal kingdom for themselves without regard to the rule of the Lord. The Tower of Babel was the symbol of their rebellion and self-sufficiency (Genesis 11:1-9). Though God did not destroy the human race, as had been the remedy used earlier,

He broke up their plot and settled them in divisive nations as a punishment for their ecumenical self-sufficiency.

## A Nation Is Born

Telescoping His sights on a more limited area of mankind, God called one man out of the cradle of civilization in Ur to be the father of a chosen people through whom "all families of the earth shall bless themselves" (Genesis 12:3 RSV). His name was Abraham and the covenant which God made with him was to be "an everlasting possession" (17:8) of the land of Canaan as the home of a select people. The long-range purpose of God was to mold and sensitize a people after His own will out of whom the "seed [of the woman]" (3:15), destined to defeat Satan, could arise. That One was to be the King who would reign in righteousness as the second Adam (1 Corinthians 15:45-47). Through Him the whole world would be restored to its primeval state which existed before the Fall.

The mills of the Lord grind slowly. After three hundred years the descendants of Abraham found themselves in bondage in the land of Egypt. Their hard lot there for over four hundred years taught them how to face hardship. Eventually, when God was ready to deliver them, He chose Moses to be the human instrument of negotiation with Pharaoh. The miracles which the Lord manifested by Moses, especially the bloodbath on the night of the Passover (Exodus 12), would convince them of the power of their God and their dependence on Him. In the defeat of Pharaoh's intent to restrain the Hebrews from leaving , and throughout the forty years of wilderness wandering after the Exodus, Moses was the mediator chosen by God to speak for the Lord and to intercede for the people. Already, the problem of creating a nation of faithful men was beginning to appear. Murmuring, questioning, complaining, disbelief – this was why it took forty years to get from Egypt to Canaan!

At Sinai it was necessary to initiate laws by which the new

kingdom would live (Exodus 20). It was the divine intention that this new endeavor would result in "a kingdom of priests and an holy nation" (19:6). For this reason the laws of the Mosaic covenant were given. In the keeping of these laws coupled with their devoted service to God, the Hebrews would set such an example that all nations would come to her light.

In the book of Joshua, we are told how the Lord gave the land of Canaan into the possession of the Hebrews as had been promised to Abraham nearly a millennium before. Wise men and women, known as Judges, were appointed to settle disputes and reconcile problems in the early days of the nation. It was not long, however, until the people of God demanded a king like the pagan nations around them, a desire which grew out of the dispersed conditions that developed after the Tower of Babel incident (1 Samuel 8:5). Of course, this displeased not only Samuel but God as well. It was an indication that the nation wanted to depend on human rule more than on divine rule. Such a departure from the divine design became apparent as early as the days of Gideon who, when asked by the people to be their king, replied, "I will not rule over you, neither shall my son rule over you: the Lord shall rule over you" (Judges 8:23). Nonetheless, although God was displeased, He was willing to give man a chance to assume a larger share in the handling of the nation's affairs. Thus we hear the Lord tell the people of Israel: "the Lord hath set a king over you" (1 Samuel 12:13).

First to be inaugurated as king was Saul, whose leadership degenerated to the point of personal despair and suicide (31:4). The second ruler was specially picked by God. His name was David and, under his reign, Israel was to enjoy her finest hours. The promise which God made to David reiterated the terms of the Abrahamic covenant and further established a throne in David's line which would never end: ". . . thine house and thy kingdom shall be established for ever before thee: thy throne shall be established for ever" (2 Samuel 7:16). And it was through this kingly line that the long-awaited Anointed One would ultimately come.

## God's Plan for a Kingdom Falls Apart

Israel's power and prominence began to enter into eclipse toward the end of the reign of David's son, Solomon, who became too intent on pagan alliances and a growing harem of wives and concubines. At his death, the kingdom broke apart under the uprising of Jeroboam, an Ephraimite, who set up a separate nation in the north with ten of the twelve tribes. Ahijah, the prophet, had predicted earlier that the kingdom would be divided (1 Kings 11:30-35). Jeroboam would be the first ruler of the Northern Kingdom, still to be known as Israel, with its capital at Samaria. Rehoboam, son of Solomon, continued the Davidic line in a new Southern Kingdom called Judah with its king's palace at Jerusalem.

Nineteen kings were to reign in Israel and nineteen in Judah until moral and spiritual degeneracy brought an end to the Northern confederation in 721 B.C. and to the Southern Kingdom in 586 B.C. Israel was besieged, conquered, and carried into captivity by Assyria. Judah was conquered by Babylon in a devastating defeat in which the Holy City of David (including the Temple of the Lord) was sacked and destroyed. God's plan to form a holy nation had fallen apart, but the kingdom promised to Abraham and the throne given to David were yet to survive. In His own inimitable way, God would gather a Remnant of the faithful in Babylon and return them to rebuild the Temple and the walls of Jerusalem under the leadership of Nehemiah. The kingdom, however, would "be no more until he comes whose right it is: and I will give it to him" (Ezekiel 21:27; cf. Daniel 7:13, 14; Hosea 3:4, 5; Luke 1:32, 33). One must recall, at this point, that the founding of the kingdom in the first place was to produce the King who would carry out God's plan. That King was to be Jesus, "the seed of the woman."

Following the fall of Judah, the kingdom of David, God turned the rule of the world over to four successive Gentile empires known to history as Babylon, Medo-Persia, Greece, and Rome. A detailed prediction of each of these ruling peoples is preserved for us in the second and seventh chapters of the prophetic book of Daniel. This period of Gentile rule, from the fall of Judah to the coming of Christ the second time, is called "the times of the Gentiles" (Luke 21:24). Under the Persian rule of Cyrus, the Remnant was permitted to return to Jerusalem (2 Chronicles 36:22, 23; Ezra 1:2, 3) where the little nation later struggled under the oppression of Greek dominance. Rome, who was next to control Israel, must be given credit for treating the Jewish people with great leniency in regard to their religious convictions. And it was in the midst of this situation that the Heir to David's throne was to appear.

## The Birth of A King

Seven hundred years before the birth of Jesus, the prophet Isaiah had announced, "O house of David . . . the Lord himself shall give you a sign; Behold, a virgin shall conceive, and bear a son, and shall call his name Immanuel" (Isaiah 7:14). The same prophet revealed that this child would bear the government of Israel upon his shoulder and be called "Wonderful Counselor, Mighty God, Everlasting Father, Prince of Peace." Furthermore, of His kingdom "there will be no end" and it shall be established "with justice and righteousness from this time forth and for ever more . . ." (Isaiah 9:6, 7 RSV). Micah also saw the day when, out of Bethlehem, would "come forth for me [God] one who is to be ruler in Israel, whose reign is from of old, from ancient days" (Micah 5:2).

For four hundred years the voice of the prophet had been silent in the land. The night had grown so dark that something had to happen. In fact, the entire world was, at this time in history, looking for a Savior. There could have been no period more ripe for the advent of the King. Even the sudden appearance of John the Baptist, reminiscent of the prophets of old, added to the feeling that something great was about to happen. His message was "Repent, for the kingdom of heaven is at hand" (Matthew 3:2). John was dead certain that the King was coming: ". . . he who is coming after me is mightier than I . . . His winnowing fork is in his hand, and he will clear his threshing floor and gather his wheat into the granary, but the chaff he will burn with unquenchable fire" (3:11, 12).

Just as God had spoken through His prophets of old, so it happened on that night in Bethlehem when the Holy Family had gone to be taxed in the great census. In a stable of hay came Him to whom the throne of David belonged. Through Mary, descendant of Nathan, son of David, Jesus was "the seed of the woman" promised in the Garden of Eden. And through His adopted father, Joseph, descendant of Solomon, son of David, He was the long-awaited King. Thus, the angelic hosts sang in the heavens over the stable where Jesus lay, "Glory to God in the highest, and on earth peace among men with whom he is pleased" (Luke 2:14 RSV). And lest there be any doubt about the identity of the babe, an angel said to the frightened shepherds, "Be not afraid; for behold, I bring you news of a great joy which will come to all the people; for to you is born this day in the City of David, a Savior, who is Christ the Lord" (Luke 2:10, 11 RSV).

## The King Is Refused His Throne

Everywhere Jesus went during His three years of preaching and teaching ministry, He announced the Kingdom as did John the Baptist, " . . . Repent: for the kingdom of heaven is at hand" (Matthew 4:17). When the Twelve were sent out on their mission, Jesus clearly stated, "Go nowhere among the Gentiles, and enter no town of the Samaritans, but go rather to the lost sheep of the house of Israel. And preach as you go saying, The kingdom of heaven is at hand" (Matthew 10:5-7 RSV). Luke records a similar charge given to the Seventy, a charge to announce,

"The kingdom of God has come near to you" (Luke 10:9 RSV).

On the Sunday before His Crucifixion, Jesus rode on a lowly beast into the City of David. Such a dramatic act was a clear claim to being the Messiah. Zechariah had prophesied that the Heir to David's throne would come "triumphant and victorious . . . humble and riding on an ass . . ." (Zechariah 9:9 RSV) and Matthew relates the events of Palm Sunday to that prophecy (Matthew 21:5). The crowds sensed the royal aura which surrounded the man on the donkey and shouted in masse, "Hosanna to the Son of David! Blessed is he who comes in the name of the Lord! Hosanna in the highest!" (Matthew 21:9 RSV). When the High Priest demanded whether Jesus were the Christ (Messiah or King designate), the Lord replied, "You have said so . . ." (26:64 RSV). The same answer was given to Pilate when the governor asked, "Are you the King of the Jews?" (27:11 RSV). On the titulus over the cross were inscribed the words, "THIS IS THE KING OF THE JEWS" (Luke 23:38 NIV). The Kingdom of Israel was offered that day to the Jewish nation on the condition that the people accept their King. But the people cried out, "Crucify him! . . . We have no king but Caesar!" (John 19:15 RSV). Within hours, Jesus was on the cross and the universe was furious. Thunder and lightning shattered the sky as darkness fell upon the nation. God had had enough! The veil of the Temple was torn apart, the earth trembled, rocks were shattered, and tombs were opened (Matthew 27:51-53).

A chosen people, whom the Lord had been preparing since the call of Abraham two thousand years earlier, had rejected God's best – His own Son. In so doing, they had refused their King and forfeited their last chance to restore the Kingdom to David. There could be no Kingdom without a King! It would be a long time before the Lord would come again with an offer like that, but come He would. And the next time it would be more than an offer – it would be a rule with an iron hand. James recalls the prophet's words given him by the King Himself, "After this I will return and I will rebuild the dwelling of David, which has fallen . . ." (Acts 15:16 RSV). Nothing could be clearer. The King is coming again. No one has said it better than the writer of Hebrews:

> He has appeared once for all at the end of the age to put away sin by the sacrifice of himself. And just as it is appointed for men to die once, and after that comes judgment, so Christ, having been offered once to bear the sins of many, will appear a second time, not to deal with sin but to save those who are eagerly waiting for him.
>
> Hebrews 9:26-28 RSV

The reference, of course, is to the Church who is "eagerly waiting for him" in His return with the clouds to catch away His believing disciples. This is where the translation of the Church fits into the picture. Let us look more closely now at the reason for this evacuation in light of what has been seen thus far in our running history of the Kingdom of Israel.

### An Historical Interlude

Philosophical theologians have duped multitudes of people within the institutional church into believing that the Church is a continuation of the Kingdom of Israel. This makes the Kingdom and the Church one and the same thing. Never has there been a greater deception foisted upon the followers of Christ than this. Nowhere does the Bible support such a theory nor is there even a hint of it. When one departs from the pure Word of God for the ambiguous opinions of men, he is in trouble. Philosophical theory is centered in man's judgment. Biblical theology is rooted in God's wisdom. They do not start at the same place nor do they end at the same destination.

The Church, far from being equated with the Kingdom of Israel, was completely unknown in the Old Testament. None of the prophets mention it except Daniel and he simply envisions a break in the prophetic timetable which he does not understand (Daniel 9). The Church is a mystery which the Hebrews never conceived. Thus when it came into existence on the Day of Pentecost, they neither understood it nor knew what to do about it. Jesus spoke of the unfolding mystery as "My Church" and announced to His disciples that He would "build it" (Matthew 16:18), a certainty that it was to be something brand new. Nowhere is the Church spoken of as something to be *rebuilt* or *restored* like the fallen Kingdom. Rather, it is to be built new as a kind of parenthesis between the Hebrew rejection of the Messiah and the Messiah's coming again to restore the Kingdom of Israel.

Paul deals with this *mystery* in his epistle to the church at Ephesus. He discusses the new relationship between our Lord and those who believe in Him in chapter two. But it is in the next chapter where the specific mystery is mentioned three times. This mystery has been revealed to the apostle but it " . . . was not made known to the sons of men in other generations as it has now been revealed to his holy apostles and prophets by the Spirit; that is, how the Gentiles are fellow heirs, members of the same body, and partakers of the promise in Christ Jesus through the gospel" (Ephesians 3:5, 6 RSV). Paul goes on to insist that he was commissioned to "make all men see what is the plan of the mystery hidden for ages in God who created all things; that through the church the manifold wisdom of God might now be made known to the principalities and powers in the heavenly places" (3:9, 10 RSV). Manifestly, the mystery involves the unmerited favor of God by which persons outside the covenant with Abraham were now invited to share equally with Jews. The basis on which the equality rests is belief in the Death and Resurrection of Christ as Savior and Lord (Colossians 1:24-28).

We do well to remember that the *ecclesia* is "the called out" people of Christ. When the Hebrew nation rejected the Kingdom of the Lord, God turned to the Gentiles (Greek word is *ethnoi* which means nations) with an invitation to enter into a spiritual relationship issuing in eternal life. "Simon has described to us how God at first showed his concern by taking from the Gentiles a people for himself" (Acts 15:14 NIV). The Church is a special group chosen to be "the Bride of Christ" (Revelation 21:2) who will share the rule of the Bridegroom when He comes to reign during the Millennium. Being the Bride, the Church is under grace, not under law as were the Jews who were citizens of a kingdom. The Bride will be members of the family of God sharing the glory of the ruling Son. This being so, the translation of the Church is necessary in order to consummate the marriage and be prepared for the resumption of the Messianic Kingdom.

Long ago Daniel envisioned a break in the dealings of God with the Davidic Kingdom (Daniel 9:24-27). He saw the entire period of Israel's history from the date of the rebuilding of the city of Jerusalem, in the fifth century before Christ, to the reign of Antichrist. The prophetic reference is to a total of seventy weeks (*shebua* in Hebrew meaning seven, thus each week equals seven years) which gives a total of four hundred ninety weeks. On the basis of events which have transpired, each of the weeks further represents a year in time. Sixty-nine weeks clearly covered the period from the rebuilding of the city to the first advent of Christ. Between week sixty-nine and week seventy there was envisioned a time when the Messiah would be "cut off." This is the rejection of the King by the Jews, His Crucifixion, and the attendant tragedies which befell the nation by the time of its final collapse in A.D. 70. It represented the prolonged period of the Church interlude which began with the death of the Savior. At the end of the Church age, Daniel sees a final week of terrible events in the life of the nation. These events, under a false Messiah, are undoubtedly the same as those described in Revelation (chapters 11-21) as the seven years of great tribulation in the reign of Antichrist.

## The Nations Are Offered Atonement

For two thousand years, the world has been in the midst of the Church age, the period between the last two prophetic weeks which is of undetermined duration. How much longer it can last no one knows, not "even the angels of heaven, nor the Son, but the Father only" (Matthew 24:36 RSV). Increasing fulfilment of biblical signs of the end would indicate that "the times of the Gentiles" are about to run out. Soon the Lord will appear and remove His Church. That will bring an end to the Church age. While it lasts, however, the saving grace of our Lord Jesus Christ is accessible for the nations.

Nowhere in the Old Testament covenant was the Gentile provided an atonement for sin. Atonement was for the Hebrew nation alone and it was sought by the High Priest on one special day during each year. Only then did he enter into the Holy of Holies to sacrifice for the people. When the veil which shrouded that holy place was rent, as Christ died on the cross, notice was given to the whole world that any man – Jew or Gentile – now had access to God through Christ's sacrifice (Hebrews 7:25-27). The sacrificial system had come to its end for Christ was "the Lamb of God who takes away the sin of the world" (John 1:29 RSV). Isaiah foresaw that sacrificial work when he wrote of the Suffering Servant, He is "like a lamb that is led to the slaughter" (Isaiah 53:7 RSV). And the Corinthian letter of Paul insists that "our paschal lamb has been sacrificed" (1 Corinthians 5:7 RSV).

Devout Jews had trusted their High Priest to obtain forgiveness for them as they obeyed God's demand for a sacrifice of blood, a symbol of returning the life to the Creator from whence it came. Christ became both man's High Priest and the sacrifice as He died upon the cross. This is the carefully explained message of the letter to the Hebrews. Atonement is now available for all people as a result of that day of Atonement observed two millennia ago. During this twenty-century interval of time, men and women, whether Jew or Gentile, need only to trust our High Priest who has obtained forgiveness for us by the sacrifice of Himself. This is what is so significant in Paul's classic challenge to the jailer: "Believe on the Lord Jesus Christ and thou shalt be saved" (Acts 16:31).

This is the meaning and purpose of the interlude in prophetic history known as the Church age or "the times of the Gentiles." God has been *calling out* a people for Himself who will be the Bride for His Son. The Ephesian letter sums up in beautiful fashion the divine plan for the mystery of the ages, the Church of our Lord.

> Christ loved the church and gave himself up for her [a reference to what God *has done* in the death of the Savior], that he might sanctify her, having cleansed her by the washing of water with the word [a clear statement about what he is *now doing* during this Church age], that he might present the church to himself in splendor, without spot or wrinkle or any such thing, that she might be holy and without blemish [a precise explanation as to what He *will do* for the Church at the translation].
>
> Ephesians 5:25-27 RSV

When the allotted time for the Gentiles is ended and the task of the Church is completed, God will say, "Everybody out!" With no reason for any more delay, the righteous dead will come out of their graves and the living believers will come out of the world order. It will be the grandest "coming-out-party" in history when Jesus presents His Bride to the Father for divine approval and blessing. That is the "blessed hope" (Titus 2:13 ) for which the Church has been looking since the Ascension of its Lord. Today, as never before, we are hearing the words of the Lord Jesus, "Surely I am coming soon." And to His words we respond, "Amen. Come Lord Jesus!" (Revelation 22:20 RSV).

## The Nature of the Church After the Rapture

The Church has nothing to do with the Kingdom of Israel.

During this time of grace, we who are Christians are to witness to both Jew and Gentile of the saving power of Jesus Christ. We are to "go . . . and make disciples of all nations" (Matthew 28:19 RSV) that the Church may finally be complete at the coming of the Lord. But the Church will never be a part of the actual Kingdom of Israel. The two are totally different and mutually exclusive. And since the *ecclesia* (the called out) have not been included in the Abrahamic covenant nor have they shared in the rejection of a Kingdom, it stands to reason that they will not figure in the troubles destined for the final days of the Jewish nation. It is certain that the State of Israel, which was reestablished in 1948, will face the most severe troubles in its ancient history. The troubles, according to prophecy of both Old and New Testaments, will engage the entire world and result in the final battle of Armageddon and the end of the age. Therefore, if the Church is to be spared this "time of Jacob's trouble" (Jeremiah 30:7; cf. Zechariah 13:8, 9), it is needful that the Lord remove it from the scene.

Several references are made in the gospels to "the marriage supper of the Lamb" (Revelation 19:9). The parable of the ten virgins is definitely Messianic and eschatological (end time) and has to do with the privilege to be enjoyed by the Church after the *parousia* (Matthew 25:1-13). There is also a story about a king who "gave a marriage feast for his son" (Matthew 22:1-14 RSV). Certainly, the motif of the Church as "the Bride of Christ"" and the many similar references to a marriage feast belong together. Our Lord is coming for His Church and together we will enjoy the festivities of the marriage supper during the interval of Antichrist's rule upon the earth. The scene is depicted aptly for us by John.

Let us rejoice and exult and give him the glory, for the marriage of the Lamb has come, and his Bride has made herself ready; it was granted to her to be clothed with fine linen, bright and pure – for the fine linen is the marriage of the Lamb has come, and his Bride has made herself ready; it was granted to her to be clothed with fine linen, bright and pure – for the fine linen is the righteous deeds of the saints. And the angel said to me, Write this: Blessed are those who are invited to the marriage supper of the Lamb.

Revelation 19:7-9 RSV

After the troubles on earth are past and the marriage supper is ended, our Lord Jesus Christ will return to the earth "with all his saints" (1 Thessalonians 3:13) where they will enjoy the thousand-year reign with Him who is the Prince of Peace. But during that seven years of awful tribulation on the earth, the redeemed will spend their time in heavenly places as those who experience one grand and glorious time of feasting, festivity, and fellowship with Christ and each other. One can only imagine what it will be like to experience this "homecoming with dinner on the ground" where the joys of reunion last, not just all day, but seven years!

# Chapter 5

# A World in Trouble

*The Absence of the Church Confounds the World*

When we speak of troubles after the evacuation, we are not thinking of the Church. Those hard times which have beset the Christian community will be over. Here on the earth, however, troubles will have just begun. The conditions on the earth will revert to a situation similar to that which existed prior to the Great Flood when there was no mediator between God and man and when the earth was steeped in corruption and violence. If the disorder and violence, revolution, and anarchy of our time seem threatening to us, then we had better not think about the future or we shall succumb to heart failure! Life in the world will grow rapidly worse – like a mounting crescendo – until the end comes.

In every generation since the days of Christ, the Church has served as the conscience of society. Often the conscience has been weak due to the degenerate state of the ecclesiastical institution. But, at least, such an institution has reminded men and women of the need for ethics and responsibility toward God and one's fellow men. What is even more important than that, in the midst of times of deep apostasy, there have always been a few who stood tall for God. In the presence of these people of God, the world has been held in check against a kind of open wickedness which would have prevailed in its absence.

Christians are "the salt of the earth" (Matthew 5:13). It is they who keep the world from going completely bad. There is a purifying quality about redeemed members of the Body of Christ which serves as a cathartic for the poison being spread through masses of fallen men in high places. To use another analogy, true Christians are like leucocytes in the body which fight against infection. When the Church is kept disease free by an unrelenting refusal to compromise, the whole world benefits. Few would argue that the Church has not been responsible for preserving the world from destruction long overdue for our wickedness. In a very real way, the true Church has restrained the hand of divine judgment on a deserving planet of rebellious creatures. Chaos and irrevocable destruction would have come long ago if the Christian Church were not at work as a purifying and preserving agent.

Jesus further emphasized that His disciples are to be "the light of the world" (Matthew 5:14). On numerous occasions in the past, we have witnessed the darkness of evil as it settled upon the world's peoples. One period in history is remembered as The Dark Ages, and even the period called The Enlightenment was filled with nether gloom due to our tragically false concept of the nature of man. But the darkness witnessed in the years now gone was as the noonday sun compared to the midnight forces to be unleashed upon the earth following the evacuation of the world by the Church. Jesus was the world's "true light" (John 1:9). When He was crucified, darkness fell upon the nation of Israel for three hours in the middle of the day. During the interval of time while the Lord is away from the earth in the flesh, Christians are charged with the responsibility of being the light! And when the Church is finally removed, the light will be gone completely! Manifestly, we are talking about the light of conscience and truth. Later we will see how God restores a faint ray of hope for persons who will believe in those dark times.

Our Lord further likened the mystery of the Church age to "leaven, which a woman took, and hid in three measures of meal, till the whole was leavened" (Matthew 13:33). This simply meant that the Church is to infiltrate the world with the leavening of the gospel. Leaven is often used in an evil sense in the New

Testament (see Luke 12:1), but it can describe a good process of inner change as well. God's Church has been commissioned to preach, instruct, heal, and serve in every area of the world's life until the gospel of redemption has leavened mankind and all his organized structures. When the leaven is no more present among men, the conditions on earth will be of such hopeless nature as to bring about the total collapse of the world order — like bread without a change agent such as yeast.

For nearly twenty centuries, the Christian Church has been despised and persecuted. This is not always true in its outward manifestations of institutional life. When the organized church compromises with pagan cultural values, it is not persecuted, just ignored. But in its inward life of commitment to the saving Christ, the true Church becomes a conscience for a people bent on secular existence (living as though there is no God) and is inevitably despised. The day will come when this situation will be reversed. Once the Church is gone from man's world, multitudes will recognize what the Christian community has meant to human existence and will regret its disappearance. When newspapers from across the earth carry the story: **MILLIONS OF CHRISTIANS DISAPPEAR FROM THE WORLD,** those left behind will be destined for calamity upon calamity. The population may be considerably decreased, but those who are still here cannot possibly profit by it!

## A Continuation of the People of Israel

Numerous prophecies in the Old Testament can only be understood in light of a restoration of the nation of Israel in full Kingdom power which was not realized in the return of the Remnant from Babylon. We can only look at a few of them here. Isaiah leaves no ambiguity in our minds when he says:

> And it shall come to pass in that day, that the Lord shall
> set his hand again the second time to recover the

remnant of his people, which shall be left, from Assyria, and from Egypt, and from Pathros, and from Cush, and from Elam, and from Shinar, and from Hamath, and from the islands of the sea.

Isaiah 11:11

That sounds rather emphatic and clear. Not until the last half of the twentieth century was this prophecy fulfilled even in a remote way. In the following verse, the prophet continues, "And he shall set up an ensign for the nations, and shall assemble the outcasts of Israel, and gather together the dispersed of Judah from the four corners of the earth (Isaiah 11:12). Both the ten tribes of Israel and the Davidic Kingdom of Judah are included in this forecast and they shall be gleaned out of the nearly two thousand year dispersion "from the four corners of the earth." That must mean a general restoration involving the farthest reaches of the world. And that did not happen when the Jews returned from captivity in Babylon.

Ezekiel, in the famous story of the resurrection of dry bones, hears the Lord affirming:

And I will make them one nation in the land upon the mountains of Israel; and one king shall be king to them all: and they shall be no more two nations, neither shall they be divided into two kingdoms anymore at all . . . And they shall dwell in the land that I have given unto Jacob my servant, wherein your fathers have dwelt; and they shall dwell therein, even they, and their children, and their children's children forever: and my servant David shall be their prince forever.

Ezekiel 37:22, 25

Daniel, in his vision of the seventy weeks, sees the system of sacrifice restored to the returned nation of Israel. This would necessitate the rebuilding of the Temple. Sacrifices will be offered unto God only in such a Temple which must be erected on its original site – Mount Zion in the city of Jerusalem where the Moslem Dome of the Rock now stands. There is debate among scholars as to whether the Temple proper stood on the site of the present mosque or perhaps slightly outside its sacred precincts. In order to accomplish this feat, the Jews must be in possession of the land of Abraham including the City of David. Only in recent years has this been the case.

Jesus warns of the end times when there will be great trouble for the Jews in their own country (see Matthew 24). No amount of spiritualizing the Scriptures can justifiably read anything else into these specific predictions. The Jews will be back in their land and the nation will continue as it was when the Romans destroyed it in 70 A.D. Everything will be modernized and many of the old landmarks are destined to be destroyed in the redevelopment of an ancient city and its surrounding country. But Hebrew life, though in disbelief as regards the Messiah, will continue after nearly two thousand years of interrupted life by the interlude of the Church age.

## The World Continues under Gentile Supremacy

At the time of the brutal massacre of myriads of Jews in Jerusalem and the vicious scattering of David's people into the far distant countries of the world, the mighty Roman Empire was in control of most of the western civilized world. The next two hundred fifty years were to be a time of terrible persecution for the new phenomenon of the Christian Church. The Jews were to suffer also, but not in their land or in such cruel manner as did the Christians. For nearly two millennia, however, the children of Abraham have been envied, despised, and driven all over the world. Everywhere they have gone they have prospered, but nations have treated them as outcasts, men and women without a country until the middle of the twentieth century. During World War II over six million of them were put to death in the concentration camps of Germany.

Following the restoration of the nation of Israel, promised to Abraham as an "everlasting possession," there is to be another restoration as well. If life is to continue as though there had been no Church age interruption, the source of tension which characterized the destruction of Jerusalem in A.D. 70 must be back in force. That source of enmity was the Roman Empire. The Bible states that, in the last days, the empire of the Caesars will be restored.

Once more we must call on Daniel, the prophet whose divine inspiration and holy insight enabled him to interpret the king of Babylon's dreams. A panorama of what was to come from the prophet's day until the end of the age is preserved for us in his vision of the four beasts which emerged out of the sea (Daniel 7:1-28). There is little disagreement about the identity of the world empires symbolized by these beasts. First, he saw a lion (Babylon); second, a bear (Medo-Persia); third, a leopard (Greece); and fourth, a beast so ferocious that he could only describe its features without giving it a name (Rome). It was the last beast which ruled when Jesus was crucified and the City of David was destroyed. What Daniel predicts about the beast of Rome involves conditions which prevail until the Second Coming of Christ. In the end of the age, there are seen ten kings (represented by ten horns) as the organized confederacy of the Roman Empire which, since its expiration in the fifth century after Christ, must be restored as Israel has been reestablished in the Land of Promise.

John the Apostle, writing over a half-century after the death of Jesus, envisions the restoration of the empire of Rome in precisely the same way as did Daniel over six hundred years earlier (Revelation 17:1-18). In this chapter, the apostle also sees the apostate religious institution (depicted in "the mother of harlots") as it works in close cooperation with the pagan empire. The "seven heads" on the beast are specifically explained as "seven mountains" where the harlot is enthroned. Rome was known as "the city of seven hills." One can hardly mistake the pointed symbolism. There are "ten horns" mentioned, as in Daniel, and they clearly represent a confederation of nations within the framework of the restored empire. More detailed study will be undertaken in a later section of this book. At this point, the important thing to remember is that both the Kingdom of David and the Roman Empire are to be restored to their respective places of power for the final conflict between God and anti-God.

## History Repeats Itself

With the Church gone from the earth, we have suggested that the world will be again as it was in those days between murderous Cain and the Great Flood. Jesus warned about that awful time between the translation of the Church and the coming of the King in judgment in Matthew's gospel.

> ...as the days of Noah were, so shall also the coming of the Son of man be. For as in the days that were before the flood they were eating and drinking, marrying and giving in marriage, until the day that Noah entered into the ark, And knew not until the flood came, and took them all away; so shall also the coming of the Son of man be.
>
> Matthew 24:38, 39

The sordid picture which Jesus draws needs no additional illumination. From His graphic description can be gathered all the information we need about the way things were before the Flood. In fact, they seem to have been much like they are right now. All the people were going about their secular pursuits as though they were oblivious to the existence of God and had no inkling of a disaster like a flood. Obviously, they had grown complacent with their little game of caring for their physical appetites. Our Lord is saying that, though this may be descriptive of almost any age to a degree, it is especially the way things will be during the tribulation. No better portrayal of life without recognition of a Supreme Ruler of the universe could be written.

Is there anything more that we can say about conditions on the earth prior to the great deluge? Probably. The Old Testament has many archetypes for persons and events later to be. In an earlier part of this book, we looked briefly at some of them. A character, usually overlooked except for his age, lived during the pre-Flood period and seems to figure in it in a rather subtle way. His name was Methuselah and his nine hundred sixty-nine years had a prophetic meaning. Methuselah's father, Enoch, was the only godly man of his day – so godly that he was translated from earth to heaven. When he named his son, he chose a word which summed up his expectations for his boy. In Hebrew the name means: "When he is gone, so be it."

It is not too much to conjecture that, in those long walks together, God revealed to His servant what was soon to happen. If so, Enoch probably asked when the flood could be expected and the Lord said, "Methuselah", a reference to Enoch's son. Thus the boy became a sign of the end. When Methuselah was gone, the Flood would come. We have sparse details about these antediluvians, therefore, we can only assume that Enoch told his son and Methuselah became an object lesson to the people who lived in the surrounding area. The news was bound to have gotten out by word of mouth until everybody knew about old Methuselah. Perhaps they laughed at the whole idea as they mocked the stupidity of old Noah who would build a huge boat in the middle of dry land.

Some will insist that all this is conjured speculation. The interesting thing is to be found in the way things worked out. Methuselah was 187 years old when his son, Lamech, was born

(Genesis 5:25) and Lamech was 182 years old when Methuselah's grandson, Noah, was born (5:28). Thus Methuselah was 369 years old at the birth of Noah. In chapter seven, where the Flood is recorded, we discover that Noah was 600 years old when the Flood came. Methuselah lived to be 969 years old. That means that he reached that hoary age the same year as the Flood destroyed the inhabitants of the old world. Apparently, he had been named right and he was a sign to the people. When he was gone, they should have gotten ready for the deluge. But they paid no attention to the sign.

Does history repeat itself? God has destroyed the world only once and He will do it only once more. The unknown writer to the Hebrews hears God saying, "Yet once more I shake not the earth only, but also heaven. And this word, yet once more, signifieth the removing of those things that are shaken, as of those things that are made, that those things which cannot be shaken may remain." (Hebrews 12:26-27). As Methuselah's removal from the earth's living was a sign to the people of Noah's day, so the translation of the Church is a sign to men and women left on the earth after the lift-off! When the Church is gone, so be it! Swift judgment will fall upon all peoples and within one prophetic week (seven years), the King will return with His saints to destroy the wicked and establish His reign of peace.

## A Political Dream Come True

First, it was the Tower of Babel. In our day it has been the League of Nations and now the United Nations. In each case, plus many attempts between the construction of the ancient Tower and World War I, man sought to create some kind of world government by which peace could be assured and every nation could be kept in line with a well-defined charter. Billions of dollars are spent each year trying to avoid war by peaceful negotiations supervised by a complex body of representatives from many countries of the world. It may be true that the United

Nations has forestalled a nuclear war and the destruction of civilization. This we will never know. It is clear that this world body has been engaged in numerous armed conflicts, using menacing implements of war, to intimidate sovereign nations in the name of peace! This inconsistency alone is enough to betray the fact that the United Nations has not eliminated war or brought a solution to the big problem which confronts the world – man himself!

Occasionally, we hear someone say that what the confused and shattered world needs now is a beneficent dictator who will rule with an iron hand. That kind of gentleman is getting to be a rare breed. But if this is what we want, we are in for a shock. For a dictator is exactly what we are going to get, only he will not turn out to be the kind we expected. According to the Scriptures, in the end of the age there will arise one man who will be demanded by the multitudes as the sole ruler of the whole earth. We will have our dictator and he will be the Antichrist. Both the Old Testament and the New foresaw his rise to power. John writes, ". . . and power was given him over all kindreds, and tongues, and nations" (Revelation 13:7).

Daniel envisioned the power of this one ruler who will control the whole restored Roman Empire comprised of its ten participating nations.

> I considered the horns, and behold, there came up among them another little horn [the Antichrist], before whom there were three of the first ten horns plucked up by the roots: and behold, in this horn were eyes like the eyes of man, and a mouth speaking great things.
>
> Daniel 7:8

Little question remains but that the United Nations – a modern Tower of Babel which seeks peace without God – is laying the necessary groundwork for the one-world government, the reins of which the coming Antichrist will easily pick up. This is not to say that the United Nations is all bad. But it is to say that man's rebel attempt to create one world without due regard to the need of a Savior to change his heart is futile. And it is further to affirm that what is taking place before our eyes is the direct fulfilment of prophecy. God said it would happen because He knows fallen human nature.

It is the complexity of a world which reels to and fro like a drunken man that has brought us to the threshold of not only accepting but demanding a dictator. Anyone who thinks more than superficially will instantly recognize the impossibility of having any semblance of world government without such an all-powerful ruler. In the vision of John, where the Antichrist is portrayed as a beast in like manner as in Daniel, these unmistakable words assure us that we may anticipate the coming of this one-world government with a bestial head.

> And the ten horns which thou sawest are ten kings, which have received no kingdom as yet; but receive power as kings one hour with the beast. These have one mind, and shall give their power and strength unto the beast.
> Revelation 17:12-13

## An Economic Dream Come True

Under the headship of the Antichrist shall develop a worldwide system of buying and selling which is carefully controlled. No one will be able to engage in business except as he is permitted by the dictator's regime. Daniel writes, " . . . he shall cause craft to prosper" (Daniel 8:25). The Book of Revelation has some very frightening things to say about the economic conditions which will prevail under the ten-nation confederacy governed by an iron-fisted dictator.

> He causeth all, both small and great, rich and poor, free and bond, to receive a mark in their right hand, or in

their foreheads: And that no man might buy or sell, save
he that had the mark, or the name of the beast, or the
number of his name.

Revelation 13:16-17

This restored Roman Empire (over which Antichrist holds sway)
will naturally be in the continent of Europe. That is where the old
empire was, with its palace and headquarters in Rome, and we
may be sure that the revived confederacy of nations will be
located there. Several attempts have been made to unify
Europe under a totalitarian form of government. Adolf Hitler is
remembered best by modern man for his efforts in this direction.
But there has never been any design for European unification in
history to compare with the European Union (earlier called the
Common Market) of our time. The plan is to have at least ten
nations within the confederacy, countries bound together in an
economic unity which would give these nations of the restored
empire the edge over any other part of the world in controlling
the economy in its own way.

It was following the Treaty of Rome in 1957 that the Common
Market came into being. Not to be overlooked is the fact that
the treaty was *signed in Rome.* It sought to bring about
economic oneness and political unity. Some of the countries
which join the European Union may later seek to withdraw.
Others will probably seek to be admitted. But if this European
effort succeeds (and there is every reason to believe that it will),
we should not be surprised to find the events of Daniel and
Revelation coming to pass very soon. We must remember,
however, that the evacuation of the Church must take place first.
And since that is so, there is good cause to prepare ourselves for
the lift-off at any moment.

As is the case with the United Nations, so it is with the
European Union. We are not branding it all bad. It is probably
a necessity for the survival of the many small countries of Europe
faced with the pressure of totalitarian aggression. What we are

saying is that it appears to be laying the foundation for the oppressive economic controls held in the hands of ten nations under the direct veto power of a universal dictator. Mention was made of nations wanting to withdraw. And it is not outside the realm of possibility that this may be what is meant in Daniel's vision of "three of the first horns [rulers in the confederacy] plucked up by the roots" (Daniel 7:8). These may be nations in the new Roman Empire who see the direction in which the whole thing is moving during the days after the translation of the Church. They may rebel against the policy of the Antichrist. If they do, they will simply be "plucked up" or annihilated.

## A Religious Dream Come True

In His high priestly prayer our Lord prayed, "That they all may be one; as thou, Father, art in me, and I in thee, that they also may be one in us . . ." (John 17:21). Within the last half-century, there has been a growing stampede to bring all Christian bodies together in a monolithic structure under the auspices of the World Council of Churches. It is held by many ecclesiastical leaders that, in doing so, the prayer of Jesus will be answered. One thing usually overlooked is the fact that it is God in His sovereign power who creates unity, not man in his weak and fallen nature. No amount of frenzied effort on man's part to thin doctrinal positions to a watery kind of spiritual bouillon will bring about the oneness for which Jesus prayed. In fact, structural union, which some bodies desire, has little to do with Christian unity. Structural union may be achieved (at least between consenting larger denominations), but it will be based on a theological premise so frail as to make questionable its continued identification as the "Body of Christ."

History records a time when there was only one Church. For a thousand years, no one dared to break away from the sacrosanct institution. Then men in the East decided to sever the tie and launch out on their own. Less than five hundred years later came the biggest split of all – the Protestant Reformation. All of us know what kind of "oneness" existed prior to the days of Martin Luther. It was union in the darkness of spiritual sterility. Apostasy was another name for the Church. Not until Luther braved the storm did anyone enter into a head-on collision with the most powerful and domineering organization in the world – the Roman Catholic Church. Some insist today that the Reformation was a mistake – at least far too drastic – and that the Christian community must return to a oneness similar to that which characterized the church before the sixteenth century.

We should expect to see stronger measures being taken against the local churches and independent groups who resist the ecumenical design of the World Council. But eventually, there will be one world church. If not before, certainly during the period after the lift-off of the Bride of Christ, there will be only one organizational structure of religion. A full description of this super-church is found in the Apocalypse (Revelation 16, 17) where the post lift-off church is called "a woman [sitting] upon a scarlet colored beast" and "MYSTERY, BABYLON THE GREAT, THE MOTHER OF HARLOTS AND ABOMINATIONS OF THE EARTH." Before the close of the final week of prophecy (Daniel's seventieth week), this world church will be destroyed by the Antichrist and he will set himself up as God in the Temple on Mount Zion. Paul refers to this in one of his many letters. Of the end-time ruler, he writes about the man "who opposeth and exalteth himself above all that is called God, or that is worshiped; so that he as God sitteth in the temple of God, showing himself to be God" (2 Thessalonians 2:4; cf. Revelation 17:16). All this is in keeping with the restoration of the Roman Empire in which Caesar worship was obligatory. The old paganism will be back in greater force than ever in the past. The one-government, one-economy, one-church world will finally be a reality and the proud dreams of a God-denying, Christ-ignoring people shall come true.

## A Peaceful Respite Followed by War

The first half of the final week on the prophetic calendar will be a period of peace and prosperity. This will be in the interest of the Antichrist's phenomenal rise to power. We are not told precisely how soon after the translation of the Church this world ruler will be acclaimed by every nation as supreme dictator. It may not be until near the middle of the week. But wonders shall not cease as men convince themselves that the Kingdom of Heaven has arrived under the deceptive powers displayed by the beast with the "iron feet" (Daniel 7:7) and "feet part of iron and part of clay" (2:33). At first, the Antichrist shall not be supreme except over the strongest confederacy of nations in the revived empire. Some "barbarians" will still be outside and, though enamored with the bestial dictator to the point of full cooperation, will later create much trouble for his planned kingdom of peaceful submission. These events will be treated with careful attention at a later point in our discussion.

It is the latter half of the seven years which will issue in terrible conflict between nations such as has never been witnessed. Not even our wildest dreams of a nuclear war can begin to conjure up an image of man's death and desolation as horrifying as that which will then take place. Men will cry, "Peace, peace; when there is no peace" (Jeremiah 6:14) for "When they shall say, Peace and safety; then sudden destruction cometh upon them, as travail upon a woman with child; and they shall not escape (1 Thessalonians 5:3).

To realize peace is not enough. Any absence of war which is constructed on man's ingenious devising is disappointing. Never in history has it been any different. Only during the time of Jesus' earthly life was there peace all over the world for any length of time. Unredeemed men cannot keep their treaties long without growing restless. Christ is the Prince of Peace and no lasting peace will be effected until His millennial reign. For this reason, He Himself predicted that there shall be "wars and rumors of wars" (Matthew 24:6). While it is true that the Master is here dealing with conditions during the last prophetic week, we may be certain that the prophecy is also apropos to this pre-lift-off period of deepening apostasy and self-sufficiency. If we would only recognize this basic point, we would see our peace efforts in a new light. Anyone with eyes and ears knows full well that the modern world is a tinderbox and becoming more explosive each year. The situation is certainly not getting better (as some churchmen have sought to make us believe), but worse and worse as Jesus and His disciples warned long ago.

# Chapter 6

# The World Welcomes Its Messiah

*The Deception of Appearances*

While the true Church is enjoying the marriage supper of the Lamb, and rejoicing in the rewards given them in heaven at the "judgment seat of Christ" (2 Corinthians 5:8-11), the masses left on the earth will be exulting in the hope of an earthly redeemer of the whole world. The Jews, in the nation of Israel, will be beside themselves with rapturous joy in the belief that their long-awaited Messiah has appeared at last. This prominent political figure (who has been becoming more and more popular in the years just prior to the disappearance of the Church) will be looking suspiciously like the kind of man destined to rule the earth. There is good reason to believe that Antichrist will be engaged in world affairs previous to lift-off, maybe even now known to millions of people as just another government statesman. "Let no man deceive you by any means: for that day shall not come, except there come a falling away first, and that man of sin be revealed, the son of perdition" (2 Thessalonians 2:3). The "man of sin" is the Antichrist, whose full disclosure will not be made known until the departure of the church.

Is it possible that he might now be a high ranking member of a president's cabinet or a king's adviser in world affairs? Could he be serving as an ambassador from some country where peace is praised but terrorism is practiced? Might he be a voice for brotherhood in the United Nations or a soft-spoken advocate of religious compromise in the Council of Churches? Or could this frightening figure, who will present such a convincing portrait of himself that the world will believe his lies, be as yet

unknown while awaiting his cue to march on stage?
Since he will be received as the deliverer, long-awaited by the
Jewish people, this exciting personality would be expected to be
Jewish. It must not be overlooked, however, that this false
Messiah might be of Arabic extraction. The Arabic peoples are
descendants of Abraham by Hagar and, although not among the
chosen people themselves, are destined to be an irritation to the
Hebrews. Following the birth of Ishmael (father of the Arabs),
God explained to Abraham, " . . . a father of many nations have
I made thee . . . and kings shall come out of thee" (Genesis 17:5,
6). It is not at all incredible to foresee the age-old conflict,
between the kings of the Arabic peoples and the kings of the
Israelites, brought to a gory climax in a final struggle between
the son of the slave woman (anti-Messiah) and the son of Sarah
(the true Messiah). At this point, of course, we are only
speculating as to who this false Messiah may turn out to be.
So successful will he be in settling international disputes that
the Gentiles will be determined to yield their most exalted seats
of power to him. And so beautifully will he handle the Arab-
Israeli powder keg that the Jews will believe that the heir to
David's throne has come.
His words will be smooth, his appearance regal, his bearing
like that of a god, and his diplomacy unequaled by mortal man.
With the conflict surrounding Israel seemingly ended, the Jewish
nation will thank their God for the peace and security of the
restored Kingdom. Almost anything suggested by this pretentious
redeemer of the Jews will be readily accepted. And this in spite
of Jesus' stern warning, "I am come in my Father's name, and ye
receive me not: if another shall come in his own name, him ye
will receive" (John 5:43). Of course, at this time the Hebrew
nation will still be a victim of unbelief in their Messiah who came
to earth and was rejected by them long ago.

## A Covenant of the Heart

Jeremiah foresaw the glad day, after God has finished with His chastisement of the people of Abraham, when there would be a new relationship between the Lord and the persecuted *diaspora* (scattered nation). He calls it "a new covenant," a relationship with God which will be far superior to the one broken by the wandering Hebrews while Moses was on the mount, and later reflected in their Lawgiver's symbolic act when he smashed the rock on which were inscribed the Decalogue or Ten Commandments (Exodus 32:1-20). This covenant would be written on the heart rather than on slabs of stone. It is well for us to hear the prophet's own words:

> Behold, the days are coming, says the Lord, when I will make a new covenant with the house of Israel and the house of Judah, not like the covenant which I made with their fathers when I took them by the hand to bring them out of the land of Egypt, my covenant which they broke, though I was their husband, says the Lord. But this is the covenant which I will make with the house of Israel after those days, says the Lord: I will put my law within them, and I will write it upon their hearts; and I will be their God, and they shall be my people. And no longer shall each man teach his neighbor and each his brother, saying, "Know the Lord," for they shall all know me, from the least of them to the greatest, says the Lord; for I will forgive their iniquity and I will remember their sin no more.
>
> Jeremiah 31:31-34 RSV

When the Antichrist (false Messiah) has expanded his power and prestige to the point where the Roman Empire will install him as the new Caesar, one of his first acts will be to draw up a treaty with the Hebrew nation. Daniel calls this treaty "a strong covenant." Apparently, he will have been so overwhelming in his success in terminating the Middle-East conflict that all parties will agree to the treaty. With his own signature on the covenant, the governing puppets of Israel will have every reason to trust its validity and permanence. No more prestigious and forceful person in the world could be found to put his name on a treaty. An illustration of the degree to which the world's peoples have been conditioned to trust the word of one charismatic man.

A bishop was recently asked why he believes our president's involvement in peace negotiations is so necessary. He replied, "Because he's the boss of the world!" Daniel describes the actual ratification of this treaty in these words:

> And he shall make a strong covenant with many for one week; and for half of the week he shall cause sacrifice and offering to cease, and upon the wing of abominations shall come one who makes desolate, until the decreed end is poured out on the desolator.
>
> Daniel 9:27 RSV

This covenant shall assure the Jewish nation of protection against any and all aggression and the nation of Israel, still blinded in disbelief, will think of the arrangement as the fulfilment of Jeremiah's prophecy. Thus their plight will be worsened in their failure to see how the world is being duped.

## The False Messiah Is Finally Revealed

At the time of the ratification of a treaty between Israel and the Roman Empire, the end-time Caesar will reveal his true identity. This must not be construed to mean that the malicious nature, later to become so prominent in his reign, is to become recognizable at this time. On the contrary, the shrewd dictator's pattern will be to create an image of brotherly love and kindness. He will even talk piously about God and his respect for Him. Through such deceitful tactics, however, his person will gradually develop the kind of holy aura which would induce people to see him as more than a man. Something mysterious will pervade his persona and wherever he goes men will praise and adore him. At the signing of the treaty will be as good a time as any for this demonic ruler to accept the opinions of the masses and announce himself as their Messiah!

Palms will wave again in the city of Jerusalem and men will cry in great accolades of Messianic praise, "Hosanna! Hosanna! Hosanna in the highest!" At last, David will have returned to bring peace and prosperity to Israel forever. Celebrations will be held across the land and all the nations of the empire will send their greetings and congratulations. What a day it shall be. From every mouth in the Land of Promise will rise the shout, "The King is here! Our Kingdom is reborn!"

Lest there be any doubt in the minds of any, immediate orders will be issued for the rebuilding of the Temple of David on Mount Zion. The fact that the Dome of the Rock is now located there and is controlled by the Muslims of the Arabic world creates no problem. With the Arab-Israeli conflict settled and the fresh smell of peace in the air, not even Muslims will object to this move. After all, everything will be moving toward one worldwide religion based solely on the Fatherhood of God and the brotherhood of man. We are already well on our way to making this the only foundation for a religious syncretism including all types of otherwise incompatible beliefs. It is possible that the suave ruler will convince all people that the only way to insure peace is through a unified religion which would bind the empire together. That is exactly the tactic used by the Caesars in the early days of Christianity. And if this is the plan, Antichrist will capitalize on the universal Fatherhood-brotherhood concept. We are already seeing the groundwork for this persuasion in the World Council and the New Age movement.

The nation of Israel will have a great thing going for them at the beginning of the last week in Daniel's prophecy. Theirs will be control of one of the richest countries in the world – rich in possessions and in tradition. After two thousand years, their land will be restored, their wandering people at peace, and their Temple rebuilt. What is even more fantastic to contemplate, their messiah will have come and it cannot be long until he establishes the throne of David again at Jerusalem. Everything will be in readiness for that glorious moment prayed for by the wailing wall for centuries. We may project a frenzied situation in which the wealthy government of Israel will begin building a palace for their messiah the moment he signs the treaty.

## Restoration of Temple Sacrifices

Once the Temple is erected on that holy mount, the system of sacrifices shall be given rebirth with bloody offerings on the altar as in the days before the Temple of Herod was demolished in A.D. 70. The whole ritual will be revived and priests will be plentiful in the land. No more will wailing be heard at the ancient wall of tears for there will be nothing to wail about. Passover feasts will still hold a high place in the Jewish year, but a new festival of *Regathering* will be instituted to mark the restoration of the land and the rebuilding of the Temple.

Lambs, bullocks, and turtle doves will abound in great numbers. No one will be so poor that he cannot provide himself with a victim of sacrifice without blemish. The welcome smell of blood in the holy precincts will be like perfume to families so long forbidden the actual blessing of temple sacrifices. Jews who do not dwell in the rejuvenated kingdom at the first will again make their annual pilgrimage to the holy mount to share in the observance of Passover and *Regathering*.

Ironic as it may be, the whole reinstated system of sacrifices is an example of traditional redundancy. Though Christ has put an end to the need for such offerings by the sacrifice of Himself on the cross, the unbelieving masses in Israel, at the outset of the final week, will not yet be conscious of this truth known to the Church for the past two millennia as a *mystery* of divine grace.

Therefore, the details of an arrangement, instituted by God as a temporary measure until the perfect sacrifice was given, will be repetitiously pursued. The whole scene will be like men desperately seeking the assurance of divine acceptance without ever coming to the knowledge that it is done.

### The Restrainer Is Removed

Let us reiterate that none of the above events can take place until the Church is gone. With the departure of the Church from the earth is also the removal of the Holy Spirit. Assuredly, the Spirit of God will always be in His world in limited fashion even during the last prophetic week. That Spirit was on earth, though faintly, during the days before the Flood. In the same way, the Third Person of the Trinity will be here during the days preceding the coming judgment in fire. But the mighty working power which came to the Church on the day of Pentecost will be withdrawn so as to allow the will of unregenerate man to show itself at its very worst.

The Apostle Paul is specific about this in the Second Thessalonian letter. He has just been clarifying the minds of his friends in relation to the rise of Antichrist which, he insists, cannot happen as long as the Holy Spirit incarnate in the Church is in the world.

> You know what is restraining him [Antichrist] now so that he may be revealed in his time. For the mystery of lawlessness is already at work, only he [Holy Spirit] who now restrains it will do so until he [Holy Spirit] is out of the way. And then the lawless one will be revealed . . .
> 2 Thessalonians 2:6-8 RSV

An interesting and illuminating observation is to be noted in the extensive account of the last prophetic week in the Book of Revelation (chapters 6-19). Not once is the New Testament word for Church (ecclesia) used by the apocalyptic narrator in these chapters. This must be because there is no true Church seen by John on the earth to be involved in this period of trouble. Likewise, while the Spirit is present in the second and third chapters, when the Church is still in the world (Revelation 2:7, 11, 17, 29; 3:6, 13, 22), and in the last chapter, which portrays the heavenly sphere in the life to come (22:7), He is conspicuously absent in the intervening chapters which depict the last week of trouble. When the Church is lifted off the earth to meet the Lord in the air, so also does the Spirit depart in His office of enduement and reinforcement reserved for the ecclesia. At that moment, Satan is free to present his Messianic substitute to the world.

### A Trinity of Satanic Rule

Satan is behind the total program scheduled for the last week in the calendar of prophecy. As his position becomes stronger (with Christ, the Holy Spirit, and the Church out of the way), the desperate adversary of man and the hater of God will no longer hide anything. For everything God does, the devil has a counterfeit. The most devilish scheme of all his deceptions is his attempt to foist on the world an unholy trinity as an imitation of the Holy Trinity of God. Satan himself will serve in the capacity of God the Father and men will be so duped and blinded by their unbelief that they will not be capable of telling the difference. John calls him the Dragon, reminiscent of the Serpent in the Creation story (Genesis 3:1), as well as Satan and Devil (Revelation 12:9, 20:2). During this time, God will have withdrawn from the world of men to let man run things in his own damning way until the time of judgment arrives. Under such conditions, Satan will have complete freedom to act the part of God and create a hell on earth.

The Second Person of the Trinity, our Lord Jesus Christ, will be counterfeited by the Antichrist called the lawless one

(2 Thessalonians 2:8 RSV), the *man of sin* and *son of perdition* (2 Thessalonians 2:3), and the *beast* (Daniel 7:7; Revelation 13:1; 19:20). He will be everything that Christ was not – evil, selfish, deceptive, and destructive. Yet, he will claim deity and perform many wondrous signs to dazzle the populace. The wonders are probably to be a combination of scientific wizardry and demonic power. His greatest feat is predicted to be some kind of fake resurrection by which he comes back to life after a mortal wound has been inflicted on his person (13:3). Whether this will be a resuscitation from what appeared to be death but was not, or an amazing demonstration of yet-to-be-discovered scientific marvel, we do not know. Whatever it is that happens, we may be sure that it will be effected by the direct power of Satan who has access to the world of evil spirits. The purpose will be to mimic the death and resurrection of Jesus and thus annul the work of God once and for all. And the people will be so overwhelmed by this spectacle as to fall down and worship him.

If Christ has a false substitute during these troubled times, so will the Holy Spirit. The Apocalypse makes reference to "the false prophet" (19:20), also called "another beast" (13:11-17), who serves as the dictator's assistant. There can be little doubt that this man is the head of the ecclesiastical organization represented by the "Mother of Harlots" (17:5) which is later destroyed by the Antichrist. Since the false prophet is still around at the judgment of the beast, we may assume that the religious head of the superchurch is kept around to serve the cause of the satanic ruler after the annihilation of his institution and liquidation of the clergy. It will be the responsibility of this false prophet to draw attention to the Antichrist, not to himself (13:12). Immediately one notes the similarity between the work of the Holy Spirit in relation to Christ and that of the false prophet in relation to the Beast. Jesus explained this work of the Holy Spirit, "When the Spirit of truth comes, he will guide you into all truth; for he will not speak on his own authority . . . He will glorify me, for he will take what is mine and declare it to you" (John 16:13,

14 RSV). Uncanny as it may seem, this is precisely what the false prophet will do for the Antichrist.

Clearly seen is the plot of deception and destruction laid out by the enemy of God. All God's works will be counterfeited. Replacing the Trinity of Father, Son, and Holy Spirit will be the Anti-trinity of Satan, Antichrist, and the false prophet. The Beast and his lying prophet will work as a team to carry out the will of their father. If Jesus said to the Pharisees, "Ye are of your father the devil . . ." (John 8:44), how much more shall those words be true of the godless pair who do the will of Satan in the end of the age!

## A Northern Invasion of Israel

About six hundred years before the coming of Christ as a babe in Bethlehem, the prophet Ezekiel envisioned a time following the restoration of Israel as a nation (Ezekiel 37:21-23) when the Land of Promise would be invaded by an armed force from the north country (chapters 38-39). Only one people live due north of the little state of Israel and that is the mammoth country of Russia. A hair-raising fact is found in studying any modern map. The city of Moscow, capital of Russia, is *directly north* of the city of Jerusalem! It is as though the two cities stand ready for the final conflict.

A number of strange-sounding place names describing specific areas in the north are employed by the prophet at a time when the Scythians were in control of the area. No such names were employed by these nomadic peoples nor had anyone heard of places by these names anywhere in the world. After six hundred years in this vast northern world, the Scythians were replaced by the Sarmatians in the third century before Christ. Still no words like those used by Ezekiel. Later came the Goths, Huns, Avars, Khazars, and Eastern Bulgars. But none of these hordes of people used the prophet's names. Then, in the ninth century after Christ, appeared the Eastern Slavs, ancestors of the modern

Russians. The founding of the Russian state is credited to Rurik who settled in Novgorod in A.D. 862. It was after this time that the names of modern Russia began to appear.

What are those place names referred to by Ezekiel fifteen hundred years before they were used? Let the prophet speak in his own words:

> The word of Jehovah came unto me saying, Son of man, set thy face toward Gog or the land of Magog, the prince of Rosh, Meshech, and Tubal, and prophesy against him, and say, Thus saith the Lord Jehovah: Behold, I am against thee, O Gog, prince of Rosh, Meshech, and Tubal . . . . Persia, Cush, and Put with them . . . Gomer and all his hordes; the house of Togarmah in the uttermost parts of the north, and all his hordes, even many people with thee.
>
> Ezekiel 38:1-6 ASV

It is concluded by biblical historians (as well as secular) and geographers that Gog and Magog refer to the far north of Russia in the area of the Caucasus mountains which still goes by the name Gogh. When the modern term Russia is rendered in Hebrew, it is the exact word used by Ezekiel and translated into English as Rosh. Moscow is the modern rendering of Meshech, the name of an early fighting tribe, and Tobolsk is named for the offspring of the northern people of Tubal. Cush is Ethiopia, Put or Phut is Libya, and Gomer is Germany. Togarmah was the son of the ancient tribal father, Gomer, and the name was preserved in the Eastern Cappodocian city of Til-garimmu referred to in the records of Assyria. Thus most of the words are place names in Russia today.

The remaining people mentioned by Ezekiel are from the Arabic world: Ethiopia, Libya, and Persia. While the powerful leadership will come from Russia in the invasion of Israel, there will be a confederacy of the north country which will include soldiers from these southern neighbors. As the Russians move down on the Land of Promise, they will be supported by an upward surge from Africa as well as a generous smattering of troops from Iran (Persia). Daniel suggests that the north country will deceitfully turn on the south and the Libyans and Ethiopians shall be crushed (Daniel 11:40-45). This would be typical of the past history of Russian alliances since the Bolshevik revolution in 1917.

Russia will invade Palestine because of the vast riches in this coveted valley of the world. At the bottom of the Dead Sea alone are mineral deposits which will make the rest of the world look like a pauper planet. Any nation who can claim these riches and bring them up from the floor of the salty sea will command the lead in the world's economy. This is His land and it is still the richest little parcel of earth in the world. Later, during the final week of prophecy, the Roman Empire will decide to ravish Israel for the same reason. It will be noticed that the Antichrist and his revived empire will not be involved in this particular invasion. The affinity between Russia and her Arabic neighbors in our time only adds to the certainty of this attack exactly as Ezekiel prophesied twenty-five hundred years ago.

The war will be the shortest in history and will end in the most devastating defeat in the annals of battle. No sooner than Russia arrives in the Land of Promise, the Lord will utterly demolish the weapons and crush the troops. Ezekiel tells it as he saw it:

> In that day there shall be a great shaking in the land of Israel. . . Behold, I am against thee, O Gog, prince of Rosh, Meshech, and Tubal . . . I will smite thy bow out of thy left hand, and will cause thine arrows to fall out of thy right hand. Thou shalt fall upon the mountains of Israel, thou, and all thy hordes, and the peoples that are with thee: I will give thee unto the ravenous birds of every sort, and to the beasts of the field to be devoured . . . And I will send a fire on Magog, and on them that

dwell securely in the isles; and they shall know that I am Jehovah. And my holy name will I make known in the midst of my people Israel; neither will I suffer my holy name to be profaned anymore: and the nations shall know that I am Jehovah, the Holy One of Israel.

Ezekiel 38:19; 39:1, 3-7

This divine intervention on behalf of the Jewish people will render the nation of Russia crippled beyond the point of ever being a contender against the Roman Empire. In fact, this crushing defeat will probably force the north country into total submission to the Antichrist's growing power. Most likely, this invasion will take place in the first half of the last prophetic week. In fact, it is probably scheduled for the early days of the post lift-off period, since the entire last week lasts only seven years and Ezekiel states that it will take that long to clean up the weapons and burn them (39:9, 10). So terrible will be the devastation of Russian troops that "seven months shall the house of Israel be burying them . . ." (39:12).

## Reduction in the World's Peoples

While it was feared by many, during the seventy year reign of Communism in the Soviet Union, that the world might someday be overrun by the godless reign of terror which threatened to bury us all, others knew that there was no chance for such a thing to happen. Now that the regime of Lenin and Mark has been thrown out, the world has grown a bit more complacent. However, the atheistic ideology is far from dead. And we can be sure that it will raise its ugly head in some guise again and again until the end of the world. Not until God says it is enough will it end. Then, in a blinding flash of judgment, it will be all over.

Not all Russians will be annihilated in the invasion. A small remnant of them will be spared to participate with the rest of the world in the Battle of Armageddon. The prophet is rather exact in his estimate of the horrible massacre: "I will turn thee back, and leave but the sixth part of thee . . ." (39:2). The Revised Standard Version omits the reference to a *sixth part* as do several translations. Many scholars feel that this verse does not allow the King James rendering but actually insists on the total destruction of Russia. The population of Russia is about 150 million, which means that this vast land is sparsely populated in comparison to the United States. Five-sixths of this number would be approximately 125 million. This would mean that, after the battle just described, the population of Russia would be suddenly decreased to a totally rural setting. While it would go practically unnoticed by the rest of the world, such a reduction in the number of people would be a major disaster for this north country.

Of interest is the fact that Joel and John both symbolize these times of judgment as an act of divine *reaping*. In his vision of the multitudes in the valley of decision at the end of the age, Joel hears God saying, "Put in the sickle, for the harvest is ripe . . ." (Joel 3:13 RSV). John later sees the fulfilment of the prophet's words in the end-time of history when Christ is seated on a white cloud with a sharp sickle in His hand. Suddenly, an angel is heard addressing Him who sits on the cloud, "Put in your sickle, and reap, for the hour to reap has come, for the harvest of the earth is fully ripe" (Revelation 14:15 RSV).

## Universal Events Are Askew

Long before the creation of man, Satan had been expelled from the place of brightness and power with God which had formerly been his. With the successful seduction of man, this archenemy of the Creator usurped the control of the earth which had been intended for Adam. Thus Satan became "the god of this world" (2 Corinthians 4:4). This does not imply that he was no longer permitted in the presence of the Lord. Job makes this clear at the outset of his drama of human suffering: "Now there was a day when the sons of God came to present themselves before the Lord, and Satan also came among them" (Job 1:6). Neither does his being "the god of this world" mean that Satan has been limited to man's earth. What this actually says is that the enemy of God and the tempter of man has access to the world for purposes of seduction and access to the dwelling place of God for the accusation of Adam's offspring.

Quite clearly, the New Testament places the headquarters of Satan and his demonic forces in the atmospheric heavens. In a figurative sense, his dwelling place is between God and man. Paul calls him "the prince of the power of the air" (Ephesians 2:2). John sees him being permanently excommunicated from both the abode of God and the atmospheric heavens in the latter days.

> And the great dragon was thrown down, that ancient serpent, who is called the Devil and Satan, the deceiver of the whole world – he was thrown down to the earth, and his angels were thrown down with him . . . . woe to you, O earth and sea, for the devil has come down to you in great wrath, because he knows that his time is short!
>
> Revelation 12:9, 12 RSV

With the translation of the Church and the withdrawal of the Holy Spirit, Satan will make his grand entrance into the world where all his forces will be loosed upon mankind. To the Church, Paul says, ". . . We are . . . contending against spiritual hosts of wickedness in the heavenly places" (Ephesians 6:12 RSV), but once the Church is gone, the arena of demonic operation will be the earth itself. Nothing will restrain the intents of Satan except in rare exceptions to be investigated later.

Naturally, with this kind of situation prevailing, one would be bound to expect the times to be out of joint. It is in light of this truth that we begin to understand what is implied in the seven

seals, seven trumpets, and seven vials of the Apocalypse (6-16).
One horrible disaster follows on the heels of the one preceding
it and each succeeding one gets worse.  Not only man is
affected but the beasts, fowl, fish, trees, vegetation, and water
feel the terrible result of man's disobedience.  The first seal (6:1,
2) reveals the arrival of Antichrist who pretends to bring peace by
carrying a bow with no arrow, but who is bent on conquering all
mankind.

At once, under the second seal, war appears in the wake of
the false Christ.  This is probably a reference to the invasion of
Israel by Russia discussed above.  Of course, this seal must
represent the many "wars and rumors of wars" during this
period.  In any event, the revelation under each seal gets worse
until the seventh which is so bad that the seven trumpeters have
to announce it in stages.   Likewise, the messages of the
trumpeters grow more terrible until the last one which is divided
into seven vials of wrath poured on the earth.  And so conditions
on the earth grow progressively more intolerable, so unbearable
that both the duped Jews and the deceived Gentiles  are in for
an unbelievable disaster.

# Chapter 7

# Half Time In The Tribulation

*The Worst Shock in Israel's History*

In Daniel's prophecy of the seventy weeks (Daniel 9:24-27), the last week, which is the time of the Antichrist, is said to be divided in the middle by a crucial development. The events described in the preceding chapter are believed, by the writer, to take place during the first three and one-half years. An exception must be made for the seals, trumpets, and vials which range across the total week.

One cannot begin to comprehend the Book of Revelation without a good grasp of the contents of the Old Testament book of Daniel. The key for interpretation of the Apocalypse is found in the prophecies of one who saw the mysteries of the Lord nearly seven hundred years before the last book of the New Testament was written. In Revelation, one encounters such expressions as "one thousand two-hundred and sixty days" (Revelation 11:3; 12:6 RSV) and "forty-two months" (11:2; 13:5 RSV). These periods of time add up to three and one-half years in each case. Furthermore, the strange expression "time, times, and half a time" is found in this vision of the Apostle (12:14). Obviously, we have the same period of time referred to here under a different analogy: "one year, plus two years, plus one-half year" equals three and one-half years. How do we know that this is the meaning of these prophetic calculations? Our clue is in the book of Daniel.

In the closing chapter of this prophecy, Daniel tells of hearing a "man clothed in linen" (clearly a divine being) inform him of the duration of the troubles which he has seen. The spokesman says that "it would be for a time, two times, and half a time; and that when the shattering of the power of the holy people comes to an end all these things would be accomplished" (Daniel 12:7 RSV). In the earlier passage to which we have often referred, the prophet writes of the last prophetic week:

> And he shall make a firm covenant with many for one week: and in the midst of the week he shall cause the sacrifice and the oblation to cease and upon the wing of abominations shall come one that maketh desolate; and even unto the full end, and that determined, shall wrath be poured out upon the desolate.
>
> Daniel 9:27 ASV

The week is seven years in length, as determined from the context and its fulfilment in history, and it is divided in the middle. Half of seven is three and one-half years.

From all this, it is apparent that something of tremendous consequence is going to transpire. It will happen in the middle of the coming seven years of satanic reign. Daniel says that the covenant made between the pagan prince and the restored nation of Israel will be broken, sacrifices stopped, and "the abomination that maketh desolate" (12:11) will be set up. In 168 B.C. Antiochus Epiphanes stopped the daily sacrifices in the Temple and built a brazen altar of an idolatrous image at which sacrifices were made to Jupiter Olympus (1 Maccabee 1:54; 6:7; 2 Maccabee 6:2). Many zealous Jews were sure that Daniel's prophecy had been fulfilled when they saw the Greek abomination of the holy place. Two centuries later, Jesus declared that this was not so. The abomination of desolation was yet to come and He warned His Jewish brethren about it.

> So when you see the desolating sacrilege spoken of by the prophet Daniel, standing in the holy place (let the

reader understand), then let those who are in Judea flee
to the mountains; let him who is on the housetop not go
down to take what is in his house; and let him who is in
the field not turn back to take his mantle . . . . For then
there will be great tribulation, such as has not been from
the beginning of the world until now, no, and never will
be.

Matthew 24:15-18, 21 RSV (See also Mark 13:14)

The events recorded in Matthew 24 and Mark 13 are all
reserved for  this calamitous period at the end of the age
predicted by Daniel and John.  When the sixth century prophet,
the first century apostle, and Jesus himself are brought together
on this matter, we discover that the story is terrifying to anticipate
but simple to interpret.   The Beast (Antichrist), who at the
beginning of the final week ratifies a treaty of peace with the
Jews and assists in rebuilding their Temple, will betray the nation
of Israel.   In the middle of the week (after three and one-half
years), he will break his covenant, desecrate the Temple, and put
an end to the Jewish system of sacrifices.

## A Pretender on the Throne in Zion

The middle of the week will be the beginning of "Jacob's
trouble" (Jeremiah 30:4-7). Incredible as it may seem to them, the
beneficent dictator of the revived empire will turn into a vicious,
murderous, insane persecutor of millions of Jews who had
become convinced that he was the long-awaited Messiah. After
waiting nearly two thousand years for the restoration of the
nation of Israel, the people of Abraham will have occupied their
Temple only two or three years when they are suddenly forced
into pagan captivity again – this time in their own land!
Antichrist will be strong enough by the middle of the week to
announce himself dictator of the whole world, not just the
Roman Empire.  Where else could he find a more appropriate

location for his capital than Jerusalem? And where in the whole world could a higher throne be found than the one in the Temple where only God is supposed to sit? Jews, Christians, and Muslims all consider that holy mount as sacred. The psychological conditioning of the minds of the masses would be electrifying.

Once he has entered the Temple and usurped the Holy of Holies for himself, the Antichrist will declare his self-inflated identity to the world over which he rules. Enamored by amazing feats of scientific and satanic power, the masses of subjects in the Gentile world will gladly accept the pseudo-deity of the Beast. The prophet, on whom we have been most dependent for our insight into this closing-out of the present world order, writes,

> . . . he shall exalt himself and magnify himself above every god, and shall speak astonishing things against the God of gods. He shall prosper till the indignation is accomplished; for what is determined shall be done. He shall give no heed to the gods of his fathers, or to the one beloved by women; he shall not give heed to any other god, for he shall magnify himself above all.
>
> Daniel 11:36, 37 RSV

Paul predicts the same action on the part of "the man of lawlessness . . . the son of perdition, who opposes and exalts himself against every so-called god or object of worship, so that he takes his seat in the temple of the Lord, proclaiming himself to be God" (2 Thessalonians 2:3,4 RSV).

Such a disgusting development of blasphemy could never happen if it were not for the obstinate rebellion and disbelief of the nation of Israel. Throughout their long history, the Abrahamic people have suffered untold anguish because they have miserably failed to live up to the great covenant given to them by God four thousand years ago. Captivity and dispersion have not succeeded in bringing them to an acceptance of the

Messiah. Only scattered instances of Jewish conversion have been recorded through the centuries. Moses warned the nation that its favored position under God would not last unless the people were faithful to the covenant made at Sinai. The consequences of their disobedience would be found in their becoming "the tail" rather than the head (Deuteronomy 28:13, 44). Nowhere does God say that He will annul the covenant, but He does warn that the result of disbelief and disobedience will be severe chastisement. The punishment continues until this day and will be culminated during the last prophetic week as the natural end of rejecting Christ and accepting the Antichrist.

### A Sealing of the Remnant

In spite of the fact that multiplied numbers of the chosen people have been murdered by anti-Semites through the centuries, it has been impossible to eradicate the sturdy stock of Abraham. Hitler was sure that he had found "a solution to the Jewish problem" in killing six million of them in five years, but he could not have been more in error in his judgment. Many of the contemporary Hebrews will be finally absorbed into the rapidly growing population of the new Israeli state.

If there is any one thing made crystal clear in the prophecies, it is that the largest percentage of these returning descendants of Abraham will continue the reconstruction of their nation in disbelief. Their Messiah will still be rejected and, in His place, they will one day accept the pseudo-Messiah as Lord and Savior. In the midst of the seven years of trouble, the Lord will deliberately raise up a cadre of Jewish witnesses who will announce the coming of the true Kingdom. This will be the Remnant chosen by Jehovah out of the massive number of descendants of Abraham who have multiplied over the centuries. Actually, what we have here is a Remnant of the remnant! John numbers them at one hundred forty-four thousand.

After this I saw four angels standing at the four corners

of the earth, holding the four winds of the earth, that no
wind should blow on the earth, or on the sea, or upon
any tree. And I saw another angel ascend from the
sunrising, having the seal of the living God: and he
cried with a great voice to the four angels to whom it
was given to hurt the earth and the sea, saying, Hurt not
the earth, neither the sea, nor the trees, till we shall have
sealed the servants of our God on their foreheads. And
I heard the number of them that were sealed, a hundred
and forty-four thousand, sealed out of every tribe of the
children of Israel . . .

Revelation 7:1-4 ASV

In the following verses, John lists the twelve tribes by name and
divides the total number of sealed witnesses into equal parts of
twelve thousand for each tribe. There is no reason not to accept
this careful divine numbering as literal. The argument of some
that none are true Jews except the descendants of Judah must be
carefully weighed. God finds faithful witnesses in each of the
tribes. And though ten tribes were lost in the Assyrian captivity,
they were not lost to God who knows where every child of
Abraham is at every moment. These witnesses will probably see
clearly what is happening in Israel as the power of Antichrist
increases.

By the middle of the time of trouble, these responsive Hebrews
will have decided that the acclaimed messiah is a counterfeit.
Small groups will begin to secretly form out of which will come
the complete number of one hundred forty-four thousand. God
will send His angel to *seal* these men prior to the godless seal
which the Beast will enforce for all people. That is, the Lord will
beat the Beast to these select Jews and brand them as His own.
The seal will be on their foreheads, which is where the Beast will
later put his mark. But, on these one hundred forty-four
thousand, the mark of blasphemy will not take. They will be
preserved from death throughout "the time of Jacob's trouble"

to witness to the coming of Christ to occupy the throne of David.

More observant readers of the Scripture will have noted that the tribe of Dan is not a part of these tribes as delineated by John. Dan was among the earliest of the tribes to go into idolatry and, for this reason, it is possible that the pseudo-Messiah may come out of this tribe (Genesis 49:17). Actually, there were thirteen tribes since Joseph's was divided between his two sons, Ephraim and Manasseh. In every list of the tribes, however, one of the groups is omitted. Usually, it is Levi, the roving priest-tribe. Here it is Dan. Also, the name of Joseph is substituted for Ephraim. Ephraim was the preferred of the two sons.

Successful beyond our imagination will be these faithful witnesses. Following the sealing of the one hundred forty-four thousand, John envisions "a great multitude which no man could number, from every nation, from all tribes and peoples and tongues, standing before the throne and before the Lamb . . ." (Revelation 7:9 RSV). They are celebrating before the throne and singing praises to God. Then John is told that "these are they which came out of great tribulation, and have washed their robes and made them white in the blood of the Lamb" (7:14). Their rewards are enumerated and insured forever. Little doubt can surround the identity of this multitude. They are the Jews and Gentiles who have been led to Christ by the one hundred forty-four thousand during the awful days of the last week of prophecy.

Certainly, the Holy Spirit will be one with these witnesses. There could be no conversion to Christ without the initiation of that Spirit. We have earlier noted that the *Paraclete* (one called to go along beside, hence the Holy Spirit) has been removed at the time of the translation. While the Spirit, as the Church has known Him since the day of Pentecost, will not be in the world during the last week, He will be here as the prophets of the Old Testament knew Him. The Spirit of God will operate again from *without* rather than from *within*. A special relationship of the

Spirit is reserved for the "Bride of Christ." It is this Spirit, which
inspired and motivated the prophets to prophesy the coming of
the Messiah, that will again be at work in the latter-day Jewish
prophets. This will be the last grand appeal of God for the
remainder of the world's peoples to repent and accept the
Lordship of Christ.

## The Explosion of Organized Humanism

Towering over the people of the modern world is a monstrous
conglomerate of ecclesiastical echelons who continue to insist
that there must be one Church. It is to be worldwide with
Catholics, Protestants, and Orthodox within its membership.
Gradually, this highly-structured organization will begin to
embrace non-Christian religions, religious groups as hostile to
each other as Judaism and Islam. In this way, it will be argued
that the Kingdom of Heaven has dawned on earth and hostilities
will be done away. The biblical foundation, for the nature and
mission of the Church, will be subtly discarded in favor of a
philosophical basis which extols the brotherhood of all people
under the loving Fatherhood of a permissive God. No theology
of any significance will be found at the center of the new and
emerging World Church. The center will be pure humanism – a
Narcissus complex in which man will love and adore himself.
Naturally, such an institution of self-love, under the disguise of
selfless religion, will be void of God and His Spirit. That fact
seems to be beside the point for myriads of churchmen today.

Young Timothy was being groomed by the Apostle Paul to
carry the torch after the martyrdom of his tutor in the faith. At the
conclusion of the second letter written to him by Paul, there are
warnings of such timely importance as to be worth quoting in this
context. The apostle is discussing the latter days as he says, "For
the time is coming when people will not endure sound teaching,
but having itching ears will accumulate for themselves teachers
to suit their own likings, and will turn away from listening to the

truth and wander into myths" (2 Timothy 4:3, 4 RSV). These words could be no more characteristic of our modern church if they had appeared in the morning newspaper. Ours is a period of deepening apostasy in segments of the institutional church. It is this apostasy which has initiated the drive to pool our weaknesses in an organization which men believe will live longer because it is big!

Let no one think that the towering religious giant, which has arisen on the horizon, is the first such tower in history. The first was begun by men and women who lived shortly after the Great Flood. It was constructed for the same reason that men are today building an ecumenical organization of religion. Anything built to the grandeur of man in the name of God is destined to collapse. The Tower of Babel was never completed. The world church of the present time is so anti-Christian, in its understanding of the purpose for which God brought it into existence, that it will suffer the same fate. Either it will be shattered before it is completed (that is, before its dreams are realized) or it will think that it has achieved its humanistic goal only to be exploded in the midst of its success.

A detailed description of the world church, existing during the first half of the prophesied last week, is given by Christ in His revelation to John on Patmos. This false church is called "the great harlot" and is pictured "sitting on a scarlet beast which was full of blasphemous names" (Revelation 17:1-3 RSV). At once we are made to understand that this prostituted institution of religion is in alliance with the Beast (Antichrist). In fact, in being depicted as *astride the Beast*, we must admit that the world church is so powerful in the early days of the end of the age as to enjoy a measure of control over the political system. Of particular interest is the contrast between this unholy alliance and the relationship between the true Church and its Messiah. The Church is the *Bride* of the Christ while the apostate church, married to the Antichrist, is a prostitute.

Throughout the Scriptures, the analogy of harlotry is employed to illustrate a relationship with God which has been broken. Idolatry (worship of other gods) is nothing other than spiritual adultery. When this world church is seen as a harlot, it is not difficult to conceive of what has happened. The harlot church has "committed fornication" with "the kings of the earth" (17:2), which means that the religious institution of that terrible time will have become the plaything of a secular, pagan world. Still claiming to be God's Church, the hierarchy and membership will be like an unfaithful wife pretending to be good only as a ruse. Religion wedded to worldliness is always harlotry.

Sometime around the middle of the week, the Beast, on which the world church has been riding, will throw off his rider. Joined by the decision of the sub-kings of the ten-nation confederacy of the rebuilt empire, the Antichrist will suddenly destroy the entire religious organization. John's words are most descriptive:

> The ten horns . . . and the beast will hate the harlot; they will make her desolate and naked, and devour her flesh and burn her up with fire, for God has put it into their hearts to carry out his purpose by being of one mind and giving over their royal power to the beast, until the words of God shall be fulfilled.
>
> Revelation 17:16, 17 RSV

What method will be used is unknown to us. From the graphic words used in this terse account, we might suspect that some form of nuclear energy will be employed to explode and burn the headquarters of the harlot. It would be done at a time when all the world church leaders were present for a summit meeting called by the false prophet himself. Thus, in one stroke, the whole thing would be obliterated forever from the earth. And let us not overlook the stated fact that this is *God's judgment* on the adulterous world church. It is only carried out by the Beast.

*The True Church Is Identified*

Revelation informs us that the Beast, on which the harlot is seen sitting, has "seven heads" and that they represent "seven hills" (17:3, 9). Though the mystery name of the harlot is "Babylon the great, mother of harlots and of earth's abominations" (17:5 RSV), we must not think of the ancient city of Babylon as being the location of the end-time church. Rather, Babylon was the symbol of the most loathsome and abominable forms of idolatry and shame. It was in the area of that city where the ancient Tower of Babel had been erected. The location is specifically said to be on "seven hills" and there is only one place in the world which has always been known by this description – the city of Rome. It stands to reason that the revived empire would have its capital in the same place as before. Rome will probably be both the capital of the political system and the headquarters of the world church until the middle of the week when the Antichrist moves his capital to the desecrated Temple in Jerusalem and destroys the ecclesiastical headquarters in Rome!

Further insight is given when John writes, "And the woman that you saw is the great city which has dominion over the kings of the earth" (17:18 RSV). What city, in its religious preeminence, has ever fitted this description except Rome? But let us look once more at the picture.

> The woman was arrayed in purple and scarlet, and bedecked with gold and jewels and pearls, holding in her hand a golden cup full of abominations and the impurities of her fornication . . . And I saw the woman drunk with the blood of the saints and the blood of the martyrs of Jesus.
>
> Revelation 17:4, 6 RSV

Manifest to all is the fact that no organization of institutional religion, at any time or any place, has ever matched the wealth, luxury, and splendor of the church at Rome. How often has the religious persecution of Christians come from Rome.

A word of caution and clarification is needed before we proceed further.  For many centuries, there have been Christians who have been bitter toward their Catholic neighbors on the assumption that the Catholic church was the harlot of Revelation. Today, as prophecy is being fulfilled before our eyes, it is becoming clear that such an assumption was not entirely correct. Many Roman Catholics are discovering the personal Christ in these days and are seeking to bring renewal to their church on the pattern of the New Testament.  This is also happening in practically every mainline denomination within Protestantism.

It is not the Roman Catholic church per se which is to become the harlot of Revelation.  Rather, it is a developing world church embracing all religious viewpoints which will ultimately be absorbed into some ultra-corrupted form of the pre-Reformation church.  Catholic-Orthodox-Protestant dialogue is making this all too obvious.  Little by little, doctrinal and theological absolutes are being thrown aside as the church moves nearer to reunion under one ecclesiastical ruler whose headquarters will be in the only reasonable place — Rome.  It is the head of that apostate church — whether called pope or doctor — who will develop into the false prophet allied with Antichrist.

When the world church is finally destroyed by the Beast, it will be due to the fact that it has served its purpose in unifying the world around a pagan, secular, atheistic dictatorship.  There will be no more need for it; therefore, the proud satanic ruler will annihilate it.  No one will be too disturbed by its demolition. The Gentiles have little respect for the ecumenical movement today and will have even less interest in it after the translation of the true Church.  Life will go on for a little while after the apostate world church is gone just as though nothing had happened.

## The Fury of an Evil Storm

Through the first three and one-half years in the last phase of the present world order, man will have observed some of history's most horrible catastrophes of nature multiplied in intensity a thousand times. The judgments revealed in the seals, trumpets, and vials stretch all across the seven years, but it is likely that the first six seals will be opened and fulfilled in the first half of the final prophetic week. Earlier we sought to identify the events under the first and second seals. The white horse and rider are the arrival of Antichrist followed by the red horse which John says means war. The third seal reveals a horse of a different color – black – and it represents famine. A natural result of war and famine is death, symbolized by the pale horse under the fourth seal. The fifth and sixth seals speak of terrible persecution against the Jews and a generalized upheaval in the forces of nature. The total picture is vividly painted in the sixth chapter of the Apocalypse.

If one is a careful student of the biblical record, he cannot have missed the amazing similarity between the seal's contents and the warning about the troubles of the end of the age as given by Jesus to the disciples in Matthew 24 (cf. Mark 13). In answer to their questions about the Second Coming of the Lord and the end of the existing world order, Jesus said essentially the same thing which John later sees on the isle of Patmos. He even follows the sequence of the six seals.

The first statement made by our Lord relating to the disciples query was, "Take heed that no one leads you astray. For many will come in my name saying, I am the Christ, and they will lead many astray" (vs. 4,5 RSV). In verses 23 through 27 are found additional remarks about these "false Christs and false prophets." The disciples are emphatically told not to believe those who cry, "Here is the Christ!" or "There He is!" They are further informed that He will not be found "in the wilderness" or "in the inner rooms" but that His Coming will be like "lightning." This simply means that no one will have to look for the true Messiah in any one place. He will be visible to all in the heavens when He returns. Included in this warning were all the precursors of the last false Messiah who would purport to be Christ across the years. John says, "The spirit of Antichrist . . . is in the world already" (1 John 4:3 RSV). The wickedness of them all will be combined in Satan's crowning effort to produce a perfect counterfeit of the Messiah.

Next, Jesus warns of coming wars (vs.6,7) revealed under the second seal in Revelation. Then comes famines (v.7) as promised in seal number three. Never in history have we seen so many famines with millions of starving people. Death (seal four) and persecution (seal five) are interwoven in a lengthy section (vs. 9-22) which includes the specific warning about the abomination of desolation. The catastrophes mentioned in connection with the sixth seal are recorded in apocalyptic fashion in verse 29. From this point in Matthew's twenty-fourth chapter, our Lord describes His return to earth and gives careful clarification as to what should be expected as signs preceding the coming in judgment. The whole chapter is at the center of the prophecies relating to the end as found in both the Old and New Testaments.

# Chapter 8

# A Full-Blown Kingdom of Man

## An End to the Separation of Church and State

By the start of the second phase of the last prophetic week on earth, the Antichrist will have everything going his way. The last vestige of ecclesiastical institutionalism will be gone and "the final solution to the Jewish problem" will appear to have been achieved. In abject fear of the demonic dictator's invincible strength and in a hypnotic state of hero worship, the world's people are by this juncture in time fully committed to the Beast. The loyal patriotism felt by the citizens of the universal kingdom of Antichrist easily comes to include an attitude of divine worship. Once again the Caesar of the revived Roman Empire sees everyone bowing and, with great emotion reminiscent of the early days of Christianity, crying, "Caesar is Lord!" Patriotism and religion – no better combination has ever been found to cement together a world which is always falling apart. And the zenith of perfection has arrived when both patriotism and worship are centered in one person.

Everybody knows quite early that the head of the world church is a powerful man. It has been noised abroad that he possesses supernatural powers like the prophets of old. The Antichrist is personally aware of this and, through the first three and one-half years, has cultivated a friendship which grows into a kind of king-advisor relationship. Together they plot the betrayal of the Jewish nation and the destruction of the world church. The understanding is that the two of them could work together much better as a team if the cumbersome institutions could be

discarded. It is in exchange for the second seat in the kingdom
that the head of the world church agrees to set up the meeting
of religious leaders in Rome where the explosion occurs.

John sees this religious personage rise "out of the earth" as
the powerful representative of the Antichrist (Revelation 13:11-18).
Its appearance is that of "another beast" with "two horns like a
lamb" and a voice "like a dragon." At once the duplicity of its
nature is observed. His appearance is a striking imitation of "the
Lamb of God who takes away the sin of the world" (John 1:29).
All through the book of Revelation, Christ is portrayed as a Lamb
(5:6; 6:1; 7:9; 12:11; 13:8; 14:1; 15:3; 17:14; 22:1; etc.) And Satan takes
advantage of the Messiah's characteristics to dupe the masses.
The strategic aspect to note, however, is that, though he tries to
look like the Lamb of God, he is actually a beast. No two
animal dispositions could be more irreconcilable. And the
clincher as to the real nature of the beast is when we hear him
speak "like a dragon." As Christ is symbolized in Revelation as
a Lamb, so Satan is portrayed as a dragon (12:3, 4, 7, 9, 16; 13:2;
16:13; 20:2). Thus we have a description of a false prophet, which
the second beast is called later (16:13), as one who tries to look
and act like the Lord but actually articulates the words and will
of Satan. That combination has deceived men and women since
the beginning of time!

The work of the false prophet is said to be that of enhancing
the reign of the Beast by building up his image in the people's
minds and drawing attention to his greatness. Pointedly, the
second beast "exercises all the authority of the first beast in its
presence and makes the earth and its inhabitants worship the
first beast . . ." (13:12). In order to do this, the Pandora's box of
demonic powers is opened by Satan and its contents are given
to the false prophet. For he will work "great signs, even making
fire come down from heaven to earth in the sight of men" (v.13).
Charisma will abound in its most evil form, and the scientific,
magic, and demonic wonders which he performs will be all but
impossible to resist. If we recall that the false prophet is the third

person of the unholy trinity and the antithesis of the Holy Spirit, we will see the reason for the use of heavenly fire. It was the Spirit of God who, on the day of Pentecost, descended with tongues of fire on the disciples (Acts 2:3). And it will be in an attempt to duplicate that powerful moment that the lesser beast manipulates the powers committed to him.

## The Idolatry of Technology

Legerdemain is the art of deceiving by sleight of hand. Everyone enjoys an evening with a good magician. We are awed and mystified by his uncanny ability to fool us. Surely, there will be some of this kind of thing involved in the work of the greatest legerdemainist ever to appear on the stage of human history. Yet, there is more to it than just magic – far more. We have witnessed in the previous century how science and technology can be either a blessing or a curse. It all depends on who uses it and how. When the marvels of our scientific and technological world get into the hands of a wild, demon-possessed, power-crazed man, the entire earth is in for trouble. In retrospect, one sees how perilously close the world came to such a fate in the nearly perfected V-2 rocket of Nazi Germany.

When the false prophet appears on the scene, he will have total control of the discoveries of scientific and technological laboratories. Combining this power with a mystic, cultic aura will be a trick the likes of which none can dream. The Scriptures say that the people will be led to make an image for the beast" (Revelation 13:14). Nothing surprising about that. How often in the past have men built images to worship? Look at the Israelites at the foot of Sinai (Exodus 32), the Egyptian's imagery in stone still observed in the ancient ruins, the huge statue erected by Nebuchadnezzar on the plain of Dura (Daniel 3), the numerous idols of the Greeks and Romans. Some of these latter gods and goddesses in stone have been found to contain conduits running under ground to the priests' quarters from which the voice of the image came to dupe the worshipers. Strikingly enough, the people in the last days will be deceived by another such talking image.

On the day when the Beast's image is dedicated in the Temple on Mount Zion (the abomination of desolation mentioned by Daniel and Jesus), the false prophet will pull off his most spectacular hoax. In the solemn ceremony attended by hundreds of thousands of excited people, suddenly the image will take on the appearance of being alive. Nowhere does the Scripture say that the image does come to life. What will happen is that the statue will move and the sound of a voice will be heard coming from it. The lifelike visage and movements of the figure, coordinated with the recorded voice, will make the sight almost eerie. With access to the wonders of science and technology, which will be far advanced by the time of the Beast, there will be no end to the numbers of ways by which the image will seem alive. And under the power of suggestion being handled by the greatest magician, wisest wizard, most capable scientist, and wickedest demon, it is normal to expect the worshiping people to believe anything.

After rejection of the truth for a long enough time, men finally get to the point where they cannot distinguish between truth and error. Jesus cautioned the Pharisees about this (Matthew 12:22-32) when they could not decide whether the Lord was doing His work by the power of God or the power of the devil. And Paul, discoursing on the days of "the lawless one" when there will be "pretended signs and wonders," flatly states, "Therefore, God sends upon them a strong delusion, to make them believe what is false" (2 Thessalonians 2:8-12 RSV). Such is the punishment deserved by men and women who refuse the truth of God and reject the light of His Son. It is no wonder that these people will believe the lies of the false prophet when they have no inner standard of truth by which to check themselves. His wonders will look so genuine, his appearance so religious. Early in His ministry, the Master warned about men like the beast "who come to you in sheep's clothing but inwardly are ravening wolves" (Matthew 7:15). That statement brings a flashback of the description of the false prophet in Revelation where he is seen with "two horns like a lamb."

## A Brand Announcing New Ownership

Working in close cooperation with the Antichrist, who dwells in sheltered security within the Temple precincts in Jerusalem, the false prophet enforces the order of the Beast that all people shall bow before the animated image. Anyone refusing to comply will be killed at once. No leniency, no trial, no mercy. The word of the dictator on Mount Zion is law — inflexible and irrevocable! Only the one hundred forty-four thousand Jewish witnesses previously sealed by God (Revelation 7:1-8; 14:1-5) will be spared.

The alternative to death will be a brand upon one's flesh similar to that inflicted on cattle grazing on unfenced lands. A brand indicates ownership and the right of the owner to dispose of his property as he wills. Once the mark of ownership has been burnt into the flesh, it cannot be removed. Henceforth, the die is cast and the marked slave has no more right to his own decisions. John envisions the brand as being infused on either the forehead or the right hand. Without the dictator's mark, one will be unable to engage in any kind of business, not even the purchase of food or clothing. Secret police will cover the earth like flies on a decaying carcass. It shall be their duty to seek out and put to death those who are disloyal.

A most illuminating explanation is given in the Apocalypse as to the meaning of the brand. The mark is a number and is equivalent to the name of the Antichrist. In one short verse, we are told to use our heads ("This calls for wisdom") and "reckon the number of the beast, for it is a human number, its number is six hundred and sixty six" (13:18 RSV). Varied and ingenious have been the suggested solutions to the proper understanding of this verse. It is a fact that numerical values were given by the Jews to each letter in the Hebrew alphabet. By adding the letters in one's name, his number could be determined. When it is remembered that the Beast in Revelation is yet future, it is recognized that knowing his name is of little significance. By the time he is announced as the world ruler, the populace will know who he is and what his name may be. To know that beforehand would change nothing since history is destined to run amuck under his reign.

To know the name is unimportant, but to know the kind of person he will be is of prime significance to the study of prophecy. Already we have seen that he is *anti*-everything that has anything to do with God. *Anti* is a prefix meaning *against* and the Beast is decidedly against Christ, the nation of Israel (though at first he deceives the Jews with a treaty), and all forms of religion. He is the antithesis of Christ, always striving to emulate Him but only under the power of a reversing demonic spirit. Christ's ministry lasted about three and one-half years and the reign of Antichrist will cover the same period of time. Christ is God, but He made Himself man. Antichrist is man, but he makes himself God. And it is at this point where the number of his name becomes extremely enlightening.

The most sacred number among the Jews was the number *seven,* This was the symbol of perfection or completion. Therefore, the Bible speaks of "seven men" to be appointed deacons in the Ancient Church (Acts 6:3), forgiving "seven times" (Matthew 18:21), "seven churches" and "seven spirits" (Revelation 1:4) and "seven angels" (15:1-6). In each instance, the perfect number suggests completion. But, especially did *seven* refer to God. What could be more perfect or complete than He? In this sense, it became a divine number for Him who created the earth in six days and rested on the seventh. For the early apostles, there was no doubt about the deity of Christ. Obviously, then, the number seven belonged to Him as well as to the Father.

Man's number was *six*. It was on the sixth day of creation that he was brought into existence. Being God's masterpiece and the highest order of earth's creatures, he deserved a place next to God. Numerically, that would have to be six if God is seven. Our first insight into the Beast's identity, then, is in discovering that the number of man is six. That is as high as he can go. But why three sixes (666)? In the Church of the New Testament era, the concept of the Trinity arose. It developed out of two facts. The Old Testament uses the plural form of the word for God by which the Hebrews insisted that all gods were summed up in the one true *Jehovah Elohim*. There was no question about God the Father in the minds of the apostles. They discovered that Jesus shared that Godhead and, shortly after His Ascension, that the Holy Spirit did as well. Thus, the God who is "three-in-one" became the Christian way of explaining God's full-orbed Being. Three is, therefore, the number of the Trinity. In light of this, God's number may be said to be 777.

We have seen, in a preceding section of our study, that Satan tries to counterfeit the Godhead during the last prophetic week with the Dragon, the Beast, and the false prophet. So we have a trinity here, too. From this it is easy enough to see what happened. Antichrist will try to be God. With every ounce of energy that he has and every deceptive strategy which he can muster, he will insist that he is divine. Even the devil-head of "three-in-one" is employed. But, alas, it does not work. He is still only a man whose number is six. And combining all the persons of his reign (Satan, Antichrist, and the false prophet) results in 666 – an extension of his power, but not an amplification of his nature into divinity. Only God is 777. Try as he will, the Beast will never usurp God's throne. Thus 666 is the number of a man – an exalted and powerful man – but still a man.

## One Last Overture of Divine Grace

Two special witnesses, in addition to the one hundred forty-four thousand, are to sound the Word of God for three and one-half years (Revelation 11:3-13). Whether this is to be in the first or the last half of the final prophetic week on earth is uncertain. It is the opinion of this writer that, since divine protection is needed, the witnesses are active in the last rather than the first part of the seven year period. It is in the last half that the tribulation becomes most severe. They are dressed in sackcloth which implies that they are pronouncing doom upon the world and calling for repentance. They are further said to be "the two olive trees and the two lampstands" (11:4), an apparent reference to the fourth chapter of the book of Zechariah. There Joshua and Zerubbabel were the witnesses nourished with divine power symbolized by the olive oil. Here, in this time of trouble, God raises up two men again to be energized by the Spirit of the Lord to proclaim the coming Kingdom and its judgment on the wicked.

From the signs which they are enabled to perform, we are inevitably led to think of Moses and Elijah who did similar things in the past. "They have power over the waters to turn them into blood, and to smite the earth with every plague . . ." (11:6 RSV). These words are strikingly familiar from the work of Moses as recorded in Exodus 7:17-19. "Fire pours from their mouth and consumes their foes . . . they have power to shut the sky, that no rain may fall during the days of their prophesying . . ." (11:5-6 RSV). That sounds precisely like the ministry of Elijah (2 Kings 1:11-12) and particularly the occasion of his restraining the rain for exactly three and one-half years (1 Kings 17:1; 18:1; cf. James 5:17-18).

As a prelude to His coming Davidic Kingdom, Jesus was transfigured in the presence of three of His disciples. In the midst of the breathtaking experience appeared Moses and Elijah (Matthew 17:3). Since they are related to the coming *parousia* in the Gospel of Matthew, there is good reason to associate them with these end-time prophets. Furthermore, Malachi said that God would send "Elijah the prophet before the coming of the great and dreadful day of the Lord" (Malachi 4:5). This prophecy must have begun to come to pass in John the Baptist who announced the first coming of the King since Jesus calls him Elijah (Matthew 17:12; Mark 9:13). However, it is reasonable to assume that the rejection of both John and Christ may demand the return of both in the end-time. One other point should be noted: Moses and Elijah stand for the best of the law and the prophets. What could be more appropriate than that the spokesmen of the law and the prophets should once again prophesy before the final realization of the Kingdom of David?

More important than their identity is their ministry and fate. Unquestionably, these two witnesses are sent as God's final appeal for men to repent. Divine patience is so inexhaustible that the Lord tries again and again. He even refuses to allow the witnesses to be killed until the three and one-half years come to an end. Beyond that point, there is no more opportunity for repentance so the prophetic witnesses are slain in the city of Jerusalem. Great joy attends their deaths and, in order to give all people a chance to see the victory of the Beast, they remain unburied for over three days. Suddenly, after three days, they are raised from the dead and ascend into heaven. Terror grips the hearts of the people as they are poignantly reminded that God will have the last word. At that moment, the land is shaken by an earthquake and seven thousand people are killed. Such earthquakes will not be uncommon in the great tribulation since nature itself will be visibly altered by the divine shaking of judgment.

## The Secular City Collapses

Continually, the world is hearing more and more about the glory of the bulging metropolis. Cities are overcrowded, dirty, polluted, and filled with wickedness and corruption. Presumably, the Creator never intended that men should live in the incredibly difficult conditions of the modern city. The first attempt to build a city was by the vagabond Cain (Genesis 4:17). Nothing is known of his success and it is possible that God brought his efforts to naught. Because of his grave sin, he was cursed to be a wanderer and a fugitive from justice. The second known attempt to create city life was connected with the erection of the Tower of Babel (Genesis 11) which was cut short by a visit from Jehovah! Later, on that spot, a city was constructed which has come to be synonymous with all that is bad about city life. It is still remembered as Babylon the Great. And it is this name which the angel gives to the political and commercial metropolis of the last days on earth. Increasingly, the model for our modern cities with their sardine-pressed populations is that of ancient Babylon. Evil permeates every facet of the big city. Crime is concentrated there and immorality becomes a way of life. In our cities is where ghetto existence becomes intolerable. Yet, multitudes continue to migrate to the urban areas in spite of the fact that we know how unwholesome they are. In the event of nuclear attack, the worst place would be in the city since the warheads would be directed to the most heavily-populated segments of society. Someday the cities will be demolished. And in their place God will construct the New Jerusalem.

The Babylon in chapter eighteen of the book of Revelation is the political and commercial center of the world in the days of the great tribulation. It, like the ecclesiastical structure by the same name, will most probably be located in Rome. All commerce will pass through its offices and be either approved or rejected by computerized processing which detects the least trace of disloyalty. Economic controls will branch out from Rome, like the arms of an octopus, to choke and restrict all political and commercial enterprises. Totally godless and devoid of conscience, every man will be for himself in a struggle to survive.

When the devastation of the city of man comes near the end of the last three and one-half years, it will be complete. The pride of science and technology will be utterly deflated forever in the holocaust which leaves the metropolis in irreparable ruins. "The kings of the earth, who committed fornication and were wanton with her, will weep and wail over her when they see the smoke of her burning" (Revelation 18:9 RSV). The merchants and seafarers from afar join their laments to that of the kings in their shock at the suddenness with which the heart of their existence has been crushed. "In one hour has thy judgment come. . . in one hour all this wealth has been laid waste" (18:10, 17 RSV).

Silence, nothing but silence, can depict the city in the wake of its cataclysmic disaster from the hand of God. The evil city is haunted by the deathly silence which John sees settle over the smoldering wasteland.

> and the sound of harpers and minstrels,
> of flute players and trumpeters,
> shall be heard in thee no more;
> and a craftsman of any craft
> shall be found in thee no more;
> and the sound of the millstone
> shall be heard in thee no more;
> and the light of a lamp
> shall shine in thee no more;
> and the voice of bridegroom and bride
> shall be heard in thee no more . . . .
> Revelation 18-23 RSV

Over the silence of earth's metropolitan doomsday will be heard the mighty voice of the heavenly throng, crying, "Hallelujah! Salvation and glory and power belong to our God . . . Hallelujah! The smoke from her goes up forever and ever . . . Hallelujah! For the Lord God the Almighty reigns" (19:1, 3, 6 RSV). Once again the population of the earth will be greatly decreased as multiplied millions perish in the corrupted city of Babylon, the revived political and commercial center of the ancient empire of the Caesars. Of course, nothing can ever so quickly curtail ecological problems as the eradication of the pollution-producing cities! Unless something is done about mankind's exploitation of the good earth by sprawling city industry and its attending contamination of earth, air, and water . . . we are destined to complete eradication.

## The Sound of Silence

The "silence in heaven for about half an hour" (8:1 RSV), which comes between the events of the sixth seal and the blowing of the seven trumpets contained in the seventh seal, probably indicates a break in the seven years of trouble.  Not only is this a brief respite arranged by a patient God, but it suggests the momentous beginning of the last half of the "time of Jacob's trouble."  Thus, we get a glimpse into judgments of far more serious consequences as the trumpets blow and the bowls of wrath are emptied (8:7-16:21).  Since the entire universe is scheduled to lose its equilibrium under the fierce sway of the satanic hordes, the tragedies depicted in these chapters are not hard to believe.  As the first trumpet blows, the earth is bombarded with a mixture of hail, fire, and blood which burns a third of the earth.  Blazing meteors are featured in the next two plagues which destroy a third of the ships at sea and poison and bloody the oceans until one-third of the fish are killed.  The fourth trumpet blast partially obscures the light of the sun, moon, and stars fulfilling the prediction of Jesus.

> And there will be signs in the sun and moon and stars, and upon the earth distress of nations in perplexity at the roaring of the sea and the waves, men fainting with fear and with foreboding of what is coming on the world; for the powers of the heavens will be shaken.
> Luke 21:25-26 RSV

The first four trumpets will be strangely reminiscent of the plagues inflicted on Egypt because of the mistreatment of the Hebrew slaves. Supposedly, these tragedies are to be leveled at the earth again for the same reason. In the remaining trinity of trumpets (referred to as woes because the judgments are pronounced against man rather than the earth and seas) human life will be viciously attacked by venomous scorpions and a demonic-empowered army of two hundred million troops who will slay a third of all humanity. If this should transpire in the near future, two billion people would die. The population explosion, which has beleaguered us in recent times, seems to become less and less of a problem.

The seventh trumpet (third woe) specifically announces an earthquake which seriously shatters Jerusalem, killing seven thousand Jews and driving masses of frightened citizens into the mountains. Assuredly, there is a relationship here to the words of Jesus, " . . . let those who are in Judea flee to the mountains" (Matthew 24:16) and "The days are coming when they will say . . . to the mountains, Fall on us; and to the hills, cover us" (Luke 23:29-30). It is possible that the mountains referred to may be the old capital of Edom across the Jordan River, a rock citadel known as Petra which was formerly a notable fortress. Nestled in the natural rock formations, where a city had been carved out of stone and housed by Edomites and Nabataens, the fleeing Jews would have the best chance of hiding.

Involved in the third woe announced by the seventh trumpet are seven bowls of wrath to be poured out on the world. Followers of Antichrist will contract a malignant disease which will produce loathsome pustules on their flesh. All ocean life dies and even the rivers and springs of fresh water become red with blood. With no water to drink, the sun's heat will blister mankind. Darkness will follow, perhaps because of an eclipse. In preparation for an invasion of Israel from the east, the Euphrates River will dry up and the Battle of Armageddon will be only days away. The hail which crumbles mighty buildings is probably associated with the destruction of political and commercial city life and the divine victory in the Valley of Megiddo. The population problem will soon be over.

# Chapter 9

# World War III

*Never Again!*

Unanimous agreement prevailed among men of state from every civilized nation on earth that there must never be another world war. That was in 1945 when the last so-called global conflict was suddenly ended with explosions of the atomic bomb over two Japanese cities. The bombing was so inhumane in its widespread destruction that even scientists were shocked by what they were seeing. Buildings disintegrated and human bodies disappeared like released gas in the heart of the explosion. Solid steel melted as if it were wax held over a flame. Where once had been a modern city, nothing remained except the blackened earth and scattered traces of rising steam. An entire city had become a cemetery – a ghost town of the past. Great numbers of people in outlying areas were killed or permanently affected by the swirls of radioactive dust. For many years to come, the soil itself would be damaged in its ability to function. Even children, born to men and women who had gone through the tragedy at its outer fringes, would be crippled or mentally maimed due to their parents' radioactive impairment.

World War II was to be the war to end all wars. Humanity could never afford another. Every major nation and numerous small countries, while still tinkering with nuclear weaponry, continue to negotiate through international channels in an effort to avoid cosmic nuclear war. Yet, entering the technological weapons race are nations formerly considered backward and technologically deprived. No longer underdeveloped, they now have the ability to launch a vicious nuclear attack. Nuclear testings continue and arsenals keep on growing, often under pretense of cooperating with all attempts to control such threatening endeavors. All over the globe, we have seen small-scale wars break out, some of them dragging into many years and involving the loss of many lives and an expenditure of exorbitant amounts of money. Innocent women, children, and the aged have suffered untold anguish and suffering in these wars. Starvation is not an abnormal state for the populace of any such nation on whose soil war is pursued.

Every precaution has been taken to insure that these small-scale wars do not escalate to a frenzied pitch which could precipitate the use of nuclear energy by some capable and despotic ruler. This could be one of the countries engaged in the battle, an uninvolved country which does no more than supply weapons, or a nation completely detached but who decides to take advantage of an opportune moment to become ruler of the world. Everyone who begins to comprehend the horrors of nuclear war is convinced that a third global war is out of the question. It would be the end of everything.

## A Future Filled with Dread

According to the Scriptures (which have never yet been proved wrong), man will be incapable of keeping the peace which he so fervently seeks. The reason is plain to see. Peace among nations is an outward sign of an inward condition. No amount of peace planning and talking can substitute for the civil war which goes on inside the hearts of men. Man, in his unregenerate state, is seething with tension and friction stimulated by unfulfilled desires. This is what causes conflicts between neighbors and finally between nations. James puts it well: "What causes wars, and what causes fightings among you? Is it not your passions that are at war in your members? You desire and do not have; so you kill. And you covet and cannot obtain; so you fight and wage war . . ." (James 4:1, 2 RSV). To work for international peace when personal peace is lacking is like holding back the steam in a pressure cooker with an airtight lid. Eventually, the top will blow!

The theology which has usurped the throne for many years, in the nineteenth and twentieth centuries, insists that the world is getting better and better. All one needs is two eyes to know that this old humanism is built on a false foundation. No one in his right mind could think that the situation in the world is improving. The reason this humanistic optimism is collapsing like a house of cards is because it failed to seriously consider the Word of God. When a concept of life is constructed on man's philosophy rather than on revealed truth, it is doomed for failure. For awhile, such sugarcoated promises encourage mankind to develop its vast potential through an intensive exposure to science and education. Usually, a sizeable crowd joins the idolatrous worshipers of man's ego-image. It becomes the popular way. Then the sweet bubble bursts in the prickly world of human sin and everybody wonders where we went wrong.

Had we been more intent across the years on knowing what the prophetic Word of God has to say, we would have spared ourselves much heartbreak and disillusionment. Very few people today have any sensible understanding of biblical prophecy. This is because our present generation has grown up on a religious and secular diet which lacks one of the vitamins essential to wholeness. We are obese with man's wisdom but frail and anemic where it really counts. If we had only taken Jesus seriously, we would never have expected the world to get better. Referring to the last events on earth prior to His return in judgment, He clearly explains:

> And you will hear of wars and rumors of wars; see that you are not alarmed; for this must take place, but the end is not yet. For nation will rise against nation, and

kingdom against kingdom . . . this is but the beginning
of the sufferings.              Matthew 24:6-8; Mark 13:7, 8 RSV

Throughout the writings of the Hebrew prophets, one is struck
again and again by the repetitious predictions of an earth-
shattering war at the end of time which will involve all the
peoples of the earth. Of such specific character are these words
that one can only think of all past wars as having been child's
play. Zechariah writes of that war:

> On that day I will make Jerusalem a heavy stone for all
> the peoples; all who lift it shall grievously hurt
> themselves. And all the nations of the earth will come
> together against it.
>
> Zechariah 12:3 RSV

With the poetic flare of a Hebrew prophet, this sixth century writer
elaborates on the particulars of the world event which he has just
described,

> In the whole land, says the Lord,
> two thirds shall be cut off and perish,
> and one third shall be left alive.
> And I will put this third into the fire,
> and refine them as one refines silver,
> and test them as gold is tested. . . .
>
> Zechariah 13:8, 9 RSV

The devastation and death will be so unbelievable in this last
conflict, in which all nations are engaged, that over 65 percent
of the world's population will be killed. It must be remembered
that the teeming peoples of the world will already have been
greatly decimated. But it will be this last battle that will solve the
problem of overpopulation once and for all time.

*Man Lights the Fuse*

As the kingdom of man nears the final stages of its existence, it will begin to fall apart. Puppet kings in the north, south, and east will grow restless with the ominous things happening everywhere. Even the subject rulers of the revived Roman Empire (there may be only seven left by this time – Daniel 7:8) shall have become so restive in their suspicion that the Antichrist, snug in his Temple in Jerusalem, has betrayed the world that they will rise up in revolt. Under a kind of obsession for self-destruction, the nations will pour fuel on their distrust of each other. Disunity will prevail in the ranks. Men everywhere will be grumbling because the promises of brotherhood and prosperity, offered to them early in the last prophetic week, have been gradually broken. No one shall know for certain who should be blamed for the shambles that characterize the world. Thus every nation will suspect its neighbor, and the spark which creates all wars will suddenly ignite a holocaust so gigantic that the scene will be an amplified repeat of the destruction of Sodom and Gomorrah as described in Genesis 19:24-28.

Coupled with this growing disillusionment with the kingdom of man, as brought into being by the sinfulness of human solidarity, will be an unquenchable hatred for the land of Palestine and its peoples. Some will start the rumor that the Jews, favored earlier by the dictator, are responsible for the desolation that is coming upon the nations. We have heard that kind of reasoning before. And there is a sense in which it is true since the restored State of Israel plays a leading role in this ultimate battle. Recognizing the explosive nature of the situation, and knowing that too many people are involved for him ever to exterminate them all, the Antichrist will take advantage of the rumor for selfish ends. To do so will turn the attention of the world to the despised Jews and eliminate the suspicion which some feel toward the Beast himself. Making it all appear to be his own idea, the Antichrist will declare war on the Israelites and seek again to unify his empire in a common cause.

The Jews have always stood for God and His intrusion in the world in the minds of men and women who despise the way of righteousness. In every attempt to destroy the Hebrew people, there has been an underlying, subtle attack upon God. In this light, the final cosmic war must be seen as the long-planned confrontation between the kingdom of man – championed by Satan and the Kingdom of God – championed by the Lord Christ. Long ago the psalmist foresaw this conflict coming when he penned in graphic words:

> Why do the nations conspire,
> and the peoples plot in vain?
> The kings of the earth set themselves,
> and the rulers take counsel together,
> against the Lord and his anointed, saying
> "Let us burst their bonds asunder,
> and cast their cords from us."
>
> Psalms 2:1-3 RSV

The spark is a twofold thing, growing out of disenchantment with the decaying utopia of man's ingenuity and deception, and the release of centuries of anti-Semitism in the hearts of the world's last generation of citizens. With a burning hatred of God, there is always a smoldering hatred of men. Where this is the situation in its most intensified form since the beginning of the human race, global war is inevitable.

### Divine Conquest Advances Quietly

Let none of us forget that our God is sovereign. Nothing takes Him by surprise nor does any man or nation do anything without divine permission. This is not to say that the Eternal God is responsible for the mess into which we get ourselves and our world, but it is to affirm dogmatically that nothing can ever happen unless He allows it. This is His universe and He is in charge. Satan and his emissaries are permitted to go only so far with their plans (cf. Job 1:6-12). Man, under the influence of this Evil Spirit, will also be checked when God decides to terminate his wickedness. One of the amazing revelations of Scripture is the way in which God can turn the evil of man into the fulfilment of the divine plan. Man, in his rebellion, can only destroy himself – never God! When he disobeys the commands of the Lord, the only thing that is broken is the man – never the eternal laws of the universe. When Pharaoh "hardened his heart" (Exodus 8:15) against the will of Jehovah for His people, the Lord used the king's rebellion to bring glory to the divine plan of the ages. Moses states that "the Lord hardened Pharaoh's heart . .." (10:20) which can only imply that God used the Egyptian ruler's proud rejection to carry out the sovereign design of the Creator. God will have His way and He has invited man to share  in the unfolding plan. When man rejects that way of truth, he changes nothing about the ultimate design. He only chooses to be a cog in the machinery of the universe rather than a son in the House of the Lord. Precisely the same thing happened at Calvary where Satan and his followers were sure that they had defeated the plan of God. All they did in crucifying the Lord of glory was to bring about the redemption of the lost world. The cross was not Satan's idea, nor was it man's. It was God's!

Likewise, the ultimate conflict among the nations of the world, as they gather in miserable disarray to flatten the people of Israel and demolish the last trace of God from the earth, is all a part of the plan of God. One cannot read the Scriptures without seeing this impossible-to-overlook truth. None of this which will happen is what He wants. God's original plan was to create a world of righteousness and peace for man and all the creatures of the earth. But man's sin has brought into existence an evil order which must be ended. God has been more than longsuffering with mankind, both Jew and Gentile. He has even told us what the signs of the end will be so that none need be

caught unprepared.  Therefore, for those who reject the Savior
and spurn God's love, there is nothing left but disaster.  And that
disaster is as much God's doing as the cross was His idea.

Joel hears distinctly this great truth that God is involved in the
final global war when he shares the revelation that he has
received.  His words are concise and crystal clear:

> Proclaim this among the nations:
> Prepare war,
> Stir up the mighty men.
> Let all the men of war draw near,
> let them come up.
> Beat your plowshares into swords,
> and your pruning hooks into spears;
> let the weak say, "I am a warrior."
>
> Hasten and come,
> all you nations round about,
> gather yourselves there.
> Bring down thy warriors, O Lord.
> Let the nations bestir themselves,
> and come up to the valley of Jehoshaphat;
> for there I will sit to judge
> all the nations round about.
>
> Joel 3:9-12 RSV

Zechariah hears the same thing in his oracle concerning
Jerusalem and the coming universal reign of Christ on David's
throne.  God Himself is speaking:

> I will gather all the nations against Jerusalem to battle,
> and the city shall be taken and the houses plundered
> and the women ravished; half of the city shall go into
> exile, but the rest of the people shall not be cut off from
> the city.  Then the Lord will go forth and fight against

those nations as when he fights on a day of battle.

Zechariah 14:2-3 RSV

Behind the scene of destruction stands God, like the Ancient of Days, commanding the whole battle and calling every shot. It is His world, His battle, and His victory! Dare any mortal mind question the wisdom or the rightness of the acts of the Lord?

## Strategic Plans for the Converging of Troops

Just as surely as the Bible accurately predicted the place of Jesus' birth (Micah 5:2), so the prophetic Scriptures tell us precisely where this great war will be fought. Even now the Middle East is being prepared for the coming conflict. Where else could the final showdown between God and Satan possibly occur than on the holy soil of Palestine? Human rebellion will be crushed near the place where it first appeared. The traditional location of the Garden of Eden is no more than five hundred miles due east of Jerusalem. And what is much more important, it was in this area that God began to create a chosen nation with the call of Abraham from the general area of Eden. The land of Canaan (Palestine or Israel) became the seed-bed for the growing of the new covenant people. There the Kingdom began and there it will be ultimately established. The great war will be Satan's best strategy which has been in the process of being designed for four thousand years. All the stops will be pulled out and the winner will take all!

From a practical standpoint alone, the last war will have to take place in Palestine. Scientists tell us that the nations of the world are rapidly depleting their resources. Soon they will be gone. Yet, the little land of Palestine, almost untouched for the past four millennia in so far as its underground minerals are concerned, holds enough needed reserves in petroleum and chemical deposits to supply the entire world for at least another thousand years. In addition, the Jews are returning to this land with their massive wealth. Can there be any doubt that God has seen to it that the Jews are not only preserved but also made wealthy for the time of this conflict? (Cf. Isaiah 60:5-9; Ezekiel 38:11-13). Israel will be completely independent, the richest nation on earth. Is it any wonder that the world's peoples (solely from a practical viewpoint) will decide to attack this smug little land?

Joel refers to the valley of Jehoshaphat (Joel 3:12) as the site of the war of the nations. No actual valley in pre-Christian days bore this name, but it is generally agreed by biblical scholars that the reference is a figurative use of the word denoting the place of divine judgment on the nations. The precise naming of the place of battle is done by John in the Apocalypse.

> And I saw . . . three foul spirits . . . demonic spirits, performing signs, who go abroad to the kings of the whole world, to assemble them for battle on the great day of God the Almighty . . . And they assembled them at a place which is called in Hebrew Armageddon.
>
> Revelation 16:13 RSV

Armageddon is a combination of two Hebrew words: *har* (hill) and *Megiddo,* the name of a mount or city on the southern elevated edge of the plain of Esdraelon, known to history as the most famous battlefield in the land of Canaan. There Barak defeated the Canaanites (Judges 4:15) and Gideon routed the Midianites (Judges 7). There also Saul met his death (1 Samuel 31:4-8) and Josiah came to the tragic end of his life (2 Kings 23:29, 30; 2 Chronicles 35:22-24). This noted battlefield at the foot of the mountain is twenty two-miles long and about fifteen miles wide. It should be noted that, while the heart of the conflict will be in this plain designed as an ideal field of battle, the deployment of troops will cover a wide area of as much as two hundred miles (cf. Revelation 14:20).

The expression, "The Battle of Armageddon," strikes terror in the hearts of people everywhere. Little knowledge of the Bible is needed for the words to conjure images of bloodshed and massacre. People who have learned nothing of its biblical and prophetic importance are innately aware that Armageddon speaks of something more horrible than they have ever known. Scientists and military men often refer to the approach of Armageddon to describe their anticipation of fearful events to come. Even poets and novelists employ the word to depict ultimate and irreversible conflict.

## A Waterloo Awaits Man's Kingdom

Madness will possess the troops in the plain of Megiddo. John speaks of "a great earthquake such as had never been since men were on the earth . . ." (Revelation 16:18 RSV) which disrupts the strategy of battle by throwing men into a panic. If we recall the second woe under the sixth trumpet (9:13-16), we will note that an army of two hundred million men will invade Israel from beyond the dried up Euphrates River. It is interesting to note that China has been claiming exactly that number of troops ready for combat today! When the armies from the western confederacy, the north, and the south are added to this vast horde, one can imagine what pandemonium will exist. Men and implements of war will be jammed against one another only to be thrown into further disarray with an earthquake. The result can be anticipated even now. In fact, prophets saw it long ago. Zechariah says it like this, "And on that day a great panic from the Lord shall fall on them, so that each will lay hold on the hand of his fellow, and the hand of the one will be raised against the hand of the other; even Judah will fight against Jerusalem . . ." (Zechariah 14:13-14 RSV). Haggai writes of the same confusion in battle, "The horses and their riders shall go down, everyone by the sword of his fellow . . ." (Haggai 2:22 RSV).

In the general upheaval of nature accompanying the earthquake, there will be indescribable horrors from the heavens. Ezekiel, in his vision of the judgment of God upon Gog, says, "With pestilence and bloodshed I will enter in judgment with him; and I will rain upon him and his hordes and the many peoples that are with him, torrential rains and hailstones, fire and brimstone" (Ezekiel 38:22 RSV). If this is to be done to Russia and her allies in the earlier invasion during the last seven years, how much more severe may we expect the divine wrath to be when poured out upon all rebel nations combined!

The fire and brimstone which *rained* upon Sodom and Gomorrah (Genesis 19:24) was molten pitch from the bitumen pits at the rim of the Dead Sea set ablaze by the explosions of the sulphur mines in the area. Falling upon men, the burning mass completely charred all flesh. With the earthquake in the end times, there naturally will be volcanic eruptions of mighty force which can create the same conditions for the multitudes in the plains of battle at the foot of Mount Megiddo. John sees it as "great hailstones, heavy as a hundred weight [exactly what one would expect from such an earthquake and volcanic upheaval], dropped on men from heaven, till men cursed God for the plague of the hail, so fearful was that plague" (Revelation 16:21 RSV).

Man's madness, pride, and rebellion will destroy him. Even nature will war against him. In his sinful disobedience of God's commands upon his life, man has cursed the whole earth and he will eventually face his crime. Not even the elements of the universe can tolerate him forever in view of the way in which he has sought to destroy the equilibrium of the cosmos. There are certain inexorable laws of nature which cannot be disregarded without dire consequences. Thus man has created the conditions which will be his own undoing at the Battle of Armageddon.

## The Sign of His Coming

This terrible battle, which culminates a series of uprisings during the entire seven years of Daniel's seventieth week, will be brought to its end by what Jesus calls "the sign of the Son of man in heaven" (Matthew 24:30). At the appearance of this sign, all weapons will be turned in the direction of the heavens and every move will be concentrated on the new threat from the sky. Man's star war defense initiative is destined to be no more effective than children playing with toy rockets. This sign will appear at the moment of earthquakes, eruptions of earth, and falling brimstone. And it will be the last straw.

Some have conjectured that the "sign of the Son of man" will be the "lightning" (24:27) which sets the skies aglow with a supernatural light similar to that which the shepherds saw on the night of the Messiah's birth (Luke 2:9). The sign of His First and Second Advents, according to this idea, would be one and the same. It has even been speculated that the sign will be that of the cross, such as Constantine saw and by which he was convinced of victory. There is no biblical hint of anything like this at all. We are safer to assume that the sign will be the appearance of Christ Himself as Daniel portrays His coming:

> I saw in the night visions,
> and behold, with the clouds of heaven
> there came one like a son of man,
> and he came to the Ancient of Days
> and was presented before him.
> And to him was given dominion
> and glory and kingdom,
> that all peoples, nations, and languages,
> should serve him;
> his dominion is an everlasting dominion,
> which shall not pass away,
> and his kingdom one

that shall not be destroyed.

Daniel 7:13-14 RSV

Jesus says that ". . . the tribes of the earth will mourn, and they will see the Son of man coming on the clouds of heaven with power and great glory" (Matthew 24:30 RSV). The wailing will be the nation's recognition of defeat in the divine sign which they have rejected. John sees that awesome moment: "Behold, he is coming with clouds, and every eye will see him, and everyone who pierced him; and all the tribes of the earth will wail on account of him . . ." (Revelation 1:7 RSV). There will be every reason to wail. The larger portion of the world's population will be finally destroyed.

The "wine press of the wrath of God" will be trodden and blood will flow "from the winepress, as high as a horse's bridle, for one thousand six hundred stadia" (14:20 RSV). The distance is about two hundred miles and covers the whole land of Israel. In the nineteenth chapter of the Apocalypse, John sees a terrible feasting on these slain bodies by the birds of the air. And there is little question but that this is what Jesus Himself was making reference to when He said to His disciples, "Wherever the carcass is, there the *vultures* will gather" (Matthew 24:26 LB). The land of Israel will be covered with carnage and the birds of prey will be sent to clean up the human pollution.

# Chapter 10

# Come, Lord Jesus

*Not Since the Ascension!*

That grand moment for which all history has waited may be just around the next turn of events. This present world order will not end with an act of man, but with the decisive movement of God. After the long night of rebellion and apostasy is over, the curtain will rise on the most glorious sight ever witnessed by mortal man. In a flash of holy brightness, like a thousand suns rolled into one, our Lord shall return in the clouds of heaven. Everyone alive on the earth after the devastation of Armageddon will see Him as visibly as did those first disciples watch His Ascension (Acts 1:11).

How all people will be able to view Him, since the world is round, has disturbed some who are bent on allowing God no secrets at all. Maybe it will be by some modern satellite-relayed television as has been suggested by technology-oriented minds. Certainly, the God who created all things will not be dependent on any mechanical device to be seen. The Lord has His own ways of communicating and He will surely have a simple method of making Himself visible to all the world at one and the same time. One of our most disturbing weaknesses is our determination to limit God.

Christ's coming will be a return to this earth in the same body as that which was seen and touched by the apostles during the interval between His Resurrection and Ascension (Matthew 28:9; Luke 24:31; John 20:19, 29; 21:12). He will be no more a ghost at His return than He was when here among us the first time.

Scripture is plain about the kind of bodily personage we may look for at the climax of the ages. Daniel foresaw "a Son of man" (Daniel 7:13) and Jesus spoke of His coming in human terms as well (Matthew 24:30; 26:64). He will not be essentially different in the world to come than He was when walking on the earth two thousand years ago. Our Lord shall still be "fully God and fully man" with no diminution of either facet of His being.

At the Ascension of our Lord, He was "crowned with glory and honor because of the suffering of death . . ." (Hebrews 2:9 RSV). And when He returns, that is the way we shall see Him. John puts it like this: "We shall see him as he is" (1 John 3:2), which means that never again will Christ be seen as One despised and rejected. At His appearance, we will see Him as the glorified Redeemer of all believers  and the King of kings promised to David himself. His coming will be in regal splendor and divine glory and all people shall bow before His power. In robes of righteousness and royalty, our God shall appear to right the wrongs of all time and establish a totally new order of existence. Man's ersatz "new world order" will give way to the genuine thing! History's yearning for redemption and fulfilment is to be realized in the returning Lord from heaven.

## More Than Twelve Legions of Angels

If Antichrist is surrounded by fallen angels and demonic spirits (Revelation 16:13-16), Christ is accompanied by the hosts of heaven (19:14). Angels have always had a major part to play in the continuing war between good and evil. Since the fall of Satan, prior to the creations of man, this battle has been in progress. When the hour of judgment comes for men and women who are alive at the Second Coming, the Son of man will come ". . . in his glory, and all the angels with him" (Matthew 25:31). Presumably, this is the same angelic retinue as that of which Jesus spoke in the Garden of Gethsemane when He rebuked Peter for the use of his sword: "Do you think that I cannot appeal to my Father, and he will at once send me more than twelve legions of angels?" (Matthew 26:53 RSV). Paul calls our attention to the "mighty angels in flaming fire" (2 Thessalonians 1:7 RSV) who will be with the Savior at His revelation in the skies. Jude, brother of our Lord, quotes Enoch's prophecy,". . . Behold, the Lord came with his holy myriads" (Jude 14 RSV).

These angels are to be used at the return of Christ to "gather his elect from the four winds, from one end of heaven to the other" (Matthew 24:31). It seems clear, from the overall tenor of the biblical teaching relating to the end of the age, that these heavenly beings are to be used like troops under the direct command of the King. Whatever the King demands, His heavenly troops will perform.

Another group of beings will also appear with Him at the Second Advent. Through the awful years of the tribulation, the Church is to be with the Lord. The redeemed in Christ are caught up before the coming of Antichrist where they share in the marriage supper of the Lamb and receive their rewards for service rendered on earth during the Church age. The Lord of heaven will come for His Church at the time appointed and those who are in Christ by faith will be translated from this earth to the heavenly sphere. Therefore, when the Lord returns to the earth, He will come with His saints who will share, as the Bride, the glories of the Bridegroom. Zechariah envisions this truth in his early writings. In his vision of the Day of the Lord which was yet future, the prophet wrote, ". . . Then the Lord your God will come, and all the holy ones with him" (Zechariah 14:5 RSV). Paul promised the saints at Colossae, "When Christ who is our life appears, then you also will appear with him in glory" (Colossians 3:4 RSV).

To be allowed the joys of the eternal state is more than we can conceive. The thrill of being permitted to associate with the angels would be a blessing undeserved by any mortal man. But, to be admitted into "the palace of the King" as His Bride forever is beyond our most fertile imagination! And yet, that is the relationship reserved for the Church for all eternity.

## What A Day That Will Be!

To Mary and Martha, Jesus had promised, "Your brother shall rise again" (John 11:23 RSV). Indeed, he did return from the dead where he had been for four days. As far as we know, however, Lazarus was later to be the victim of death as are all men. The temporary conquest of death by Jesus in the life of this one man, was a sign to the people of His day that someday the exception would become the rule for the children of God. Christ is "the resurrection and the life" and the man "who believes in [Him], though he die; yet shall he live" (11:25). On that glorious day of our Savior's return for His people multitudes will share the new life which came to Lazarus. The difference is that it will be permanent for both him and all whose bodies await Christ's arrival.

It will not be forgotten that those who died in Christ, between the crucifixion of Jesus and the translation of the Church, will have been raised from the dead at the moment when the Lord returns for His Bride. But what is going to happen to those who accept Christ during the seven years and are killed by the Beast? Many shall seal their faith with their blood in response to the witnessing of the one hundred forty-four thousand and the two special witnesses whom God will send to announce the coming Kingdom. John saw ". . . a great multitude . . . standing before the throne and before the Lamb, clothed in white robes . . . and crying out with a loud voice, Salvation belongs to our God who sits upon the throne, and to the Lamb" (Revelation 7:9, 10 RSV). One of the elders identifies the multitudes as "they who have come out of great tribulation" (7:14). The question which arises at this point is: When do these saints arise from their martyr graves.

Later, in the reference to the binding of Satan at the Second Coming of Christ, John says of those who had been beheaded by the Beast, "They came to life, and reigned with Christ a thousand years" (20:4 RSV). This is a definite placing of the resurrection of the martyrs, of the last prophetic week, at the time of the return of the Lord with His Bride. But still we have to do something with the saints of the Old Testament who were neither a part of the Church nor among the tribulation martyrs. Isaiah promised, "Thy dead shall live, their bodies shall rise. O dwellers in the dust, awake and sing for joy!" (Isaiah 26:19 RSV). But when? Daniel offers some help. In his prophecy relating to the time of the end, especially the last seven years, he writes, "And many of those who sleep in the dust of the earth shall awake, some to everlasting life . . ." (Daniel 12:2 RSV).

Obviously, on the basis of the biblical record, both the Old Testament saints and those who are martyred for resisting the Antichrist will be raised from the dead when the Savior returns with the Church. Though separated from the resurrection of the deceased members of the Body of Christ at the translation by a period of seven years, this is still the *first* resurrection. The initial stage of this resurrection was the victory of Christ over death on the first day of the week. Second comes the translation of the Church with the rising of Christians from their places of bodily interment. Third is the resurrection of the Old Testament saints and the slain tribulation disciples at the return of Christ in judgment. All three of these stages are included in what John calls "the first resurrection" (Revelation 20:5) since *first* suggests "something before" that which follows. The second resurrection ("second death" – 20:6) is reserved for the wicked while the first includes only the righteous. Therefore, the three phases are all to be seen as distinct acts of God *in time,* but only one *in kind.* While these distinctions may seem to be meticulous in detail, an understanding of the total panorama of prophecy, as it relates to the life to come, is vitally important.

*Judgment and Blessing Comes to Israel*

As last minute preparations are made for the realization of the Davidic Kingdom as a pure theocracy, the Jews will be called together to determine who shall be permitted admittance into the thousand years of peace. The scene is pictured for us by the prophet Ezekiel.

> I will bring you out from the peoples and gather you out from the countries where you are scattered, with a mighty hand and an outstretched arm, and with wrath poured out; and I will bring you into the wilderness of the peoples, and there I will enter with your fathers in the wilderness of the land of Egypt, so I will enter into judgment with you, says the Lord God. I will make you pass under the rod, and will let you go in by number. I will purge out the rebels from among you, and those who transgress against me; I will bring them out of the land where they sojourn, but they shall not enter the land of Israel . . . .
>
> Ezekiel 20:34-38 RSV

The company of Jews included in these words is made up of those who manage to escape the scourge of the Antichrist as well as the horrors of the great battle. It would appear that this reference has a more stringent urgency than the initial return to Palestine alone. Also, Jews from all over the world will be gathered in Palestine to be judged. Paul writes to the Gentiles that "all Israel shall be saved" (Romans 11:26), but earlier in the letter he has enunciated the truth that "not all who are descended from Israel belong to Israel, and not all are children of Abraham because they are his descendants . . ." (Revelation 9:6-7). What this verifies is that all who are a part of the true Israel, by faith in the Messiah and His Kingdom, will be granted entrance into the theocratic reign. By the same token, being a Jew in the flesh alone is insufficient reason for such acceptance. Some of the peoples in the new state of Israel will have accepted their coming Kingdom and its King during the tribulation and escaped death. Their kind will be saved. And while it is their faith which saves them, their works are important enough to be surveyed and examined by the Judge.

> Then I will draw near to you for judgment; I will be a swift witness against the sorcerers, against the adulterers, against those who swear falsely, against those who oppress the hireling in his wages, the widow and the orphan, against those who thrust aside the sojourner, and do not fear me, says the Lord of hosts.
>
> Malachi 3:5 RSV

Deeds are included in the criteria for judging, not because any will be saved by works, but because one's works grow out of his faith and thus prove it. Abraham himself was saved by faith (Hebrews 11:8-10).

As they watched Him ascend from the Mount of Olives, the believing Jewish apostles were promised that their Lord would come back in the same way they had watched Him depart. The interlude of the Church age stopped the prophetic clock. When Jesus comes back for His Church, the clock will begin ticking off the last minutes of the world order as we know it. And at that moment, when He comes in judgment to establish the Kingdom of Israel as promised to the patriarchs, the King will begin at the precise point from which He took leave. Listen to the prophet of twenty-five hundred years ago explaining how it will happen:

> On that day his [the coming Christ] feet shall stand on the Mount of Olives which lies before Jerusalem on the east; and the Mount of Olives shall be split in two from east to west by a very wide valley; so that one-half of the Mount shall withdraw northward, and the other half southward.
>
> Zechariah 14:4 RSV

Known to all Bible students is the fact that the Mount of Olives has two high spots between which exists a fault or weakness which probably traces the path of the coming cataclysmic break when the Lord's feet stand again at the place from which He ascended. It is here that the judgment will take place. And it is from this sacred Mount that Christ will restore the Kingdom of Israel.

## Gentile Nations Have Their Day in Court

Our most graphic portrayal of the Lord as returning Judge is given to us by the most apocalyptic of Jesus' apostles. No longer does he see Jesus on a donkey in humiliation, but he envisions Him on a white charger riding to victory. His word picture is so well done that one must let him speak for himself.

I saw heaven standing open and there before me was a white horse, whose rider is called Faithful and True. With justice he judges and makes war. His eyes are like blazing fire, and on his head are many crowns. He has a name written on him that no one but himself knows. He is dressed in a robe dipped in blood, and his name is the Word of God. The armies of heaven were following him, riding on white horses and dressed in fine linen, white and clean. Out of his mouth comes a sharp sword with which to strike down the nations. He will rule them with a rod of iron. He treads the winepress of the fury of the wrath of God Almighty. On his robe and on his thigh he has a name written: KING OF KINGS AND LORD OF LORDS.

Revelation 19:11-16 NIV

It is manifest that the judgment in this passage is meted out to the Gentiles. Specifically, "the nations" are mentioned which makes the point clear. Furthermore, there is no question as to who the Judge is since John calls Him, "The Word of God," the name given by the same author, in the prologue to his gospel, to the articulated Being of God incarnate in human flesh (John 1:1-14).

No one can overlook the effort of Antichrist to imitate the One on "a white horse" at the outset of the last prophetic week (Revelation 6:2). The rider on the earlier white charger came promising peace while thrusting the world into war. The Rider on the latter horse comes in declared judgment in order to bring universal peace at last. The "sharp sword" with which He "smites the nations" is seen coming from His mouth. The psalmist speaks of men whose tongues are "a sharp sword" (Psalm 57:4). By that he means that their words are cutting and destructive. Likewise, the writer of Proverbs says that God's word is "sharp as a two-edged sword" (Proverbs 5:4 RSV). No further insight is needed to convince us that the instrument of judgment and destruction upon the wicked is *The Word of God* Himself! Luther had this in mind when he convincingly sang of Christ's final confrontation with Satan: "One little word shall fell him." It is that divine Word, which called all things into being, which will also inflict judgment upon evil in its every form.

Although it is abundantly true (with the Gentiles as it was with the Jews) that man will be saved by faith alone, his works have a way of expressing tangibly what his faith really is. No one more aptly captures this truth than James: "So faith by itself, if it has no works, is dead . . . I by my works will show you my faith" (James 2:17-18 RSV). Those Gentile works, which will best reveal the hearts of non-Jews toward Christ as they have lived through the tribulation, are described for us in the Master's words as recorded by Matthew. Christ is pictured sitting on His throne with the nations (Gentiles) before Him. A separation is taking place between the sheep and the goats – the sheep on the right hand of the Shepherd-King and the goats on the left. To those who are accepted by the One on the throne, the Lord explains,

> For I was hungry and you gave me food, I was thirsty
> and you gave me drink, I was a stranger and you
> welcomed me, I was naked and you clothed me, I was
> sick and you visited me, I was in prison and you came to
> me . . . . Truly, I say to you, as you did it to one of the
> least of these my brethren, you did it unto me.
>
> Matthew 25:35, 36, 40 RSV

Gentile nations who are rejected from admission to the reign of
peace are those who failed in the kind of life for which the
faithful are commended in the above words.

   Who are the Lord's "brethren"? They are the Jews! No one
could possibly fail to understand that if he has read the
Scriptures at all carefully. Thus, Jesus is insisting that one's
attitude toward the Hebrew people has an eternal bearing on his
acceptance or rejection by God. Four thousand years ago, God
assured Abraham and his descendants that the nations would
"bless themselves" or be cursed by the way they treat the chosen
people. Nations, as a whole, who have vigorously oppressed
the Jews have suffered for it. And someday, individuals will be
received into the Kingdom's reign or expelled from the presence
of the Lord on the basis of their attitude toward the Israelites.
And this is so because, in light of the emphasis of holy writ, our
unacceptable works betray our lack of saving faith! In view of
this we can better understand the strong dedication of persons
who spend their entire lives as missionaries to the Jews. There
is no finer way to fulfill the Lord's plan for the Jewish people than
by pointing them to their Messiah, even Christ the King.

   Gentiles and Jews, however, who have not turned to the Lord
as Savior and proved their faith by their service to God and their
attitude toward the Kingdom, will be slain "with the sword that
came out of the mouth of the rider on the horse. . ." (Revelation
19:21 RSV). In no way should we allow ourselves to think of our
Lord as being vicious or even harsh because of this warlike
appearance. As has been pointed out, the sword is symbolic for

the Word of God. Shortly before the cross, Jesus warned us about this day of judgment.

> As for the person who hears my words but does not keep them, I do not judge him. For I did not come to judge the world, but to save it. There is a judge for the one who rejects me and does not accept my words; that very word which I spoke will condemn him at the last day.
>
> John 12:47-48

Nothing could be clearer. No man is left in the dark about what is to come. The same Word which brings life when accepted brings death if spurned. "The word of God is quick, and powerful, and sharper than any two-edged sword . . ." (Hebrews 4:12).

## A Verdict and the Sentence

In the concluding moments of the Battle of Armageddon, the Antichrist and his confederation of vassal kings are scheduled to attack the returning Son of God. Manifestly, their carnal weapons have no power over Him who long ago conquered death and is "alive for evermore" (Revelation 1:18). Nevertheless, the attempt on His life will be made. What follows cannot be called a battle in the ordinary sense of that word. Tersely the account is given: "They will make war on the Lamb, and the Lamb shall overcome them, for he is Lord of lords and King of kings, and they that are with him are called and chosen and faithful" (17:14). How the Lamb will overcome the Beast is not told us in detail. We are only guaranteed that such will be the outcome of the agelong conflict between the forces of good and evil.

The apostle to the Gentiles has a word about the manner in which the Beast will be overcome, a suggestion fully in line with what would be expected in light of Christ's judgment on Jews and Gentiles alike. Of the Antichrist, Paul says, ". . .the Lord Jesus will slay him with the breath of his mouth and destroy him by his appearing and his coming" (2 Thessalonians 2:8 RSV). Here again is a reference to the use of the Word of God as a weapon of destruction when it has been flouted and spurned. Little difference exists between the "sword of his mouth" and "the breath of his mouth." In these words, one can sense that it is the eternal Word of Jehovah which brings about the ultimate downfall of the Antichrist.

An additional point of interest is provided in the term "captured" to describe the handling of both the Beast and the false prophet (Revelation 19:20). Military language is employed throughout the Apocalypse. Probably we are to perceive this term as a symbol of the submission of both the political and ecclesiastical powers to the immutable and unconquerable Word. When one is captured, he cannot help himself. Under such circumstances he absolutely is incapable of further resistance. Nothing is left for him but unconditional surrender. Indubitably, the divine Word will have the final authority.

Once the Beast and the false prophet are brought into submission to "the breath of his mouth" they are both "cast alive into the lake of fire burning with brimstone" (19:20). It will be recalled that brimstone can be likened to the red-hot pitch which rained down on Sodom, the wicked city of the plains in Abraham's day. In the Old Testament, the place where Christ casts the Beast and his co-worker is called *Topheth*, "a place of burning" (cf. Isaiah 30:33). This is not *Hades* (abode of the wicked dead), a temporary prison until the time of the White Throne Judgment. This is *Hell*, symbolized by Jesus as the burning dumping ground outside the city of Jerusalem (Mark 9:43-48). The fires will be stoked and ready for their first two victims. Whether the fires are literal or not is beside the point. The torment of *Hell* will be far worse than fire alone could ever be. And it will be forever.

## Satan in a Holding Pattern

Lucifer did his damage in heaven and he has ceaselessly caused havoc upon the earth. For the last half of the tribulation period, his efforts will be greatly intensified as we have seen in an earlier section of our study. His two colleagues in evil – Antichrist and the false prophet – having been cast into *Hell*, Satan will be dealt with next in the solution to the problem of evil as determined by God at the beginning of the human race. He who has been responsible for all the wickedness and heartache since the fall of Adam is to be consigned to a place of stringent restriction from which he will not be permitted to make further attacks upon the earth. His days of manipulation will be passed and his contacts shall be confined to the world of evil spirits (Jude 6). John succinctly depicts the event like this:

> Then I saw an angel coming down from heaven, holding in his hand the key of the bottomless pit and a great chain. And he seized the dragon, that ancient serpent, who is the Devil and Satan, and bound him for a thousand years, and threw him into the pit, and shut it and sealed it over him, that he should deceive the nations no more, till the thousand years were ended . .
>
> Revelation 20:1-3 RSV

With the use of the Greek term *abussos*, rendered "bottomless pit," one discovers that Satan is not cast into the same place as the Antichrist and his false prophet. They are to be in *Hell* permanently, but Satan is in the pit for one thousand years. He is not destroyed, only defeated and taken captive by the Lord Jesus Christ. His being bound with a chain emphatically affirms the sovereignty of God over His number one enemy. The pit, or abyss, is the dwelling place of the evil spirits. It is from this area of dark and foul demons that the devil marshals his vast army to defy, seduce men, and defeat Christ. At last he will be shut up in his own quarters, however, where he will have a thousand years to design a new strategy for his last invasion of the Kingdom of God. It is during this millennium of the imprisonment of Satan that the Appointed Heir to David's throne will rule in peace and righteousness over the whole earth. In the next chapter, we shall look at that joyous and exciting reign of the King of kings.

# Chapter 11

# The Blossoming Of The Kingdom Of God

*For A Thousand Years*

Can any of us even faintly conceive what the incredible blessings of a world under the direct rule of God, without the interference of Satan, shall be like? Surely, there will be great and wonderful surprises beyond our dreams. Yet, God has given us some insight in the Scriptures. He has even further granted us spiritual perception by which we just sense some things "in our bones." Paul felt this tingle up his spine as he penned those oft-quoted words, "No eye has seen, no ear has heard, no mind has conceived what God has prepared for those who love him [quoted from Isaiah 64:4] but God has revealed it to us by his Spirit" (1 Corinthians 2:9-10 NIV). In a very special way, that is true as regards our premonitions about the life to be in the Millennium.

For thousands of years, man has been trying to create a paradise out of the earth. Since the moment of Adam's rebellion, which brought a curse upon every part of God's creation, conditions have grown worse. At certain intervals in the long trek from primitive to modern man, a ray of hope has broken through and humanity predicted better things for itself. In every instance, it has been the inevitable plight of the human race to slip back into its old patterns and render its gains of no lasting significance. Hence, in our technological culture we are confronted by a world filled with evil and its damning results. Everywhere we are seeing and hearing about the determination of modern man to do away with war, poverty, and injustice. The facts do not indicate that we are being successful. Poverty is increasing, prejudice and discrimination are growing, and war seems inevitable. We have made a giant-size mess out of God's world.

By now many people are beginning to suspect that the world's only hope must come from outside man himself. Even those who have no such proneness towards a recognition of the supernatural are bemoaning the hopeless fate of the human race. A few still cling to man's *innate goodness,* with blinkers on their eyes, and argue that mortal man will yet produce an earthly utopia; but their numbers are rapidly decreasing. Regardless as to what men may think or say, we have been assured by the prophets, apostles, and Jesus Himself that God will finally step into the cosmic dilemma and set everything right. There is no biblical word more dogmatically affirmed than that.

### The Unfolding of a Divine Plan

When the Creator placed man in the primeval garden, it was the immediate plan of the divine Spirit to establish an unbroken relationship between Himself and man, by which the creature would live in peace and prosperity all his days. Falling into disobedience almost at once, Adam forced God to postpone the design for man into the future. The selection of one man to obediently found a Kingdom, in the midst of the idolatrous descendants of Adam, was a part of that long-range plan. When the people of Abraham failed in their share of the covenant, the Lord turned their existence into one prolonged period of discipline. In the interval, He called out a distinct group from the world who would enjoy a favored place in the world to come. That place would be granted purely on the basis of the faith commitment made by those people to Christ. In time, God's plan includes another round with the chosen people of a Kingdom which floundered on the shoals of disobedience. And at that time, the originally designed Kingdom of God will be established. Finally, the whole universe shall again become a paradise of the Creative Spirit. The original plan will be realized.

This has to be true lest God and His Christ are a failure. The Creator did not start something which He cannot finish. Christ is "the Alpha and Omega, the beginning and the ending . . ." (Revelation 1:8). What has been intended by a sovereign Trinity shall be culminated exactly as the Godhead wills. Not one *i* will be left without a dot nor will a single *t* be uncrossed. Although it has been a long time in coming, the promised Kingdom shall arrive. Our Savior promised this fulfilment of the divine plan even as He faced the cross. Holding in His hands the cup which symbolized His own blood, He said, "Truly I say unto you, I shall not drink again of the fruit of the vine until that day when I drink it new in the kingdom of God" (Mark 14:25 RSV.) None of the disciples fully perceived all that was wrapped up in that statement of prophecy, but not a single man misconstrued what was meant by the Kingdom yet to come.

Daniel interpreted King Nebuchadnezzar's dream, in which the king had seen an image with frightening appearance, but which was smote by a stone and destroyed. The explanation of the dream was a prophetic picture of the kingdoms of Babylon, Medo-Persia, Greece, and Rome. The latter kingdom was represented by "feet partly of iron and partly of clay" and the mountain stone, which "was cut by no human hand," struck those vulnerable feet of the image and destroyed it completely. The stone was unquestionably the Messiah and it "became a great mountain and filled the whole earth." In conclusion, the prophet exclaimed, "The dream is certain and its interpretation sure" (Daniel 2:31-45 RSV). No fact is more certain than that "the earth shall be full of the knowledge of the Lord as the waters cover the sea" (Isaiah 11:9 RSV).

## As Good As the Garden of Eden

John Milton talked about paradise *lost* and paradise *regained*. Everyone knows that we have lost it, but not everyone is aware that it can be found again. The kind of life which Adam enjoyed in the garden is a sample of what the earth will be like during the reign of Christ. Moses describes conditions prior to the fall:

> The Lord God planted a garden in Eden, to the east, and placed in the garden the man he had formed. The Lord God planted all sorts of beautiful trees there in the garden, trees producing the choicest of fruit. At the center of the garden he placed the Tree of Life, and also the Tree of Conscience, giving knowledge of Good and Bad. A river from the land of Eden flowed through the garden to water it; afterwards the river divided into four branches. One of these was named the Pishon; it winds across the entire length of the land of Havilah, where nuggets of pure gold are found, also beautiful bdellium and even lapis lazuli. The second branch is called the Gihon, crossing the entire length of the land of Cush, the third branch is the Tigris, which flows to the east of the city of Asher. And the fourth is the Euphrates.
>
> Genesis 2:8-14 LB

One can envision a perfect land where everything is beautiful and good and where there is nothing to disturb or molest the peaceful pursuit of personal fulfillment in the presence of God.

In portraying the coming of the Messiah to the Mount of Olives, Zechariah mentions the intriguing fact that "on that day living waters shall flow out from Jerusalem, half of them to the eastern sea, and half of them to the western sea; it shall continue in summer as in winter" (Zechariah 14:8 RSV). Even the waters of Eden will be brought to the Holy City where, at the present time, there is no river at all! An even more exciting prediction about these health-giving waters, free from pollution, is given by Ezekiel (47:1-12). Palestine is located at the approximate center of the world's continents and it is understandable why the healing waters should emanate from that point in the Millennium. Accompanying the fresh waters will be a renewed earth with air so pure that the soil will become abundantly productive (cf. Amos 9:13, 14; Zechariah 3:10; 8:12; Isaiah 55:13; 41:18, 19; Romans 8:19-22).

With the population problem corrected by an overwhelming reduction in people from the earth, man's life will be greatly extended. Except in rare instances of open rebellion, he will live a thousand years if present on the earth at the beginning of the millennial reign. That is longer than Methuselah! This should not surprise us when it is remembered that the One, who brought healing and strength to the diseased and infirm while on the earth the first time, will be present again to make wholeness as natural as brokenness has been. Isaiah sees the time when

> . . . the eyes of the blind shall be opened,
> and the ears of the deaf unstopped;
> then shall the lame man leap like a hart,
> and the tongue of the dumb sing for joy.
> For waters shall break forth in the wilderness,
> and streams in the desert.
>
> Isaiah 35:5-6

Still there is more. The regained paradise will be even better than the original Eden. The Tree of Conscience will still be here so that it is possible to sin, but Satan himself will not be around. To live in the Garden of Eden without the tempter is the utopia which humankind has sought so long without success. And that is due to the unavoidable influence of the devil which is now everywhere man goes and a part of all his endeavors. Utopia is God's gift to the faithful. It is never man's gift to himself. Of God's making is the Kingdom and it will come when He binds Satan and places on David's throne Him "to whom it belongs" (Genesis 49:10 RSV).

## The Dream of the Poets Fulfilled

Mankind has tried every conceivable kind of human government. Some have been better than others, but they have all had the germs of evil decay at heart. It is not long before any new approach to governing people starts to deteriorate. This is so because both the governed and the governors are sinful by nature. God has the only perfect system. We call it a *theocracy* – the ruling of man by the will of God. And this is the kind of rule we will have when Christ is on David's throne. "For the Lord of hosts will reign on Mount Zion and in Jerusalem . . ." (Isaiah 24:23 RSV) and His "people will abide in a peaceful habitation, in secure dwellings, and in quiet resting places" (32:18 RSV).

The injustice, about which men have complained since the genesis of time, shall be corrected since Christ "will rule them with a rod of iron" (Revelation 19:15). Selfishness, under the disguise of a struggle for justice, will be exposed. Men will live together in righteousness and peace when He who is at the right hand of the Father sits on His rightful throne – and the enemies of the Kingdom are "made his footstool" (Hebrews 10:13). "He shall reign for ever and ever" (Revelation 11:15) "for he must reign till he hath put all enemies under his feet" (1 Corinthians 15:25). Zechariah's prophecy will be brought to pass in its entirety when "the battle bow shall be cut off, and he shall command peace to the nations . . ." (Zechariah 9:10 RSV).

No more will hostility and fear fill the air. It is not enough to say that men will live in peace, but we must also point out that the animal kingdom in its entirety will exist in harmony. The Messianic prophet *par excellence* says it this way:

> The wolf shall dwell with the lamb,
> and the leopard shall lie down with the kid,
> and the calf and the lion and the fatling together,
> and a little child shall lead them.
> The cow and the bear shall feed;

> their young shall lie down together;
> and the lion shall eat straw like the ox.
> The sucking child shall play over the hole of the asp,
> and the weaned child shall put his hand on the adder's den.
>
> Isaiah 11:6-8 RSV (cf. Ezekiel 34:25)

In this description of the Millennium, we see restored the relationship between man and the beasts which characterized the Garden of Eden.

At last the prophecy which points to a time when there will be no more wars will be realized. A common mistake, made by persons and groups seeking peace for the nations in a sinful world, is to quote Isaiah's prophecy as though it can be fulfilled before the coming of the Lord. There is no way to have world peace until the Prince of Peace has returned to sit on the promised throne. Then, and only then, shall nations "beat their swords into plowshares, and their spears into pruning hooks ..." (Joel 3:10). It is easy to see that this prophecy has not come true in this present world order – the kingdom of man.

## One More Time Around

Men and women who survive the tribulation and gain entrance into the millennial reign with Christ will still be as human as ever. They will retain their mortal bodies and will live in families and have children. The charter members of the Kingdom will all be in complete accord with the will of Christ. Then shall come to pass that promise made by Paul to the Philippians that ". . . at the name of Jesus every knee should bow, in heaven and on earth and under the earth, and every tongue confess that Jesus Christ is Lord, to the glory of God the Father" (Philippians 2:10, 11 RSV). However, as children are born who do not know the way things were before the Son of God sat on the throne in Jerusalem, the fallen nature of humankind will begin to exert itself. For this reason the King will rule with a rod of iron. There may be an occasional attempt at rebellion but, if such should be the case, the King of righteousness will immediately put an end to it. With the glorified Church reigning with Him and the heavenly hosts serving as His defenders of state, the world will experience the kind of *good dictatorship* it desired in its deceived worship of the Antichrist.

Across the thousand years there will be growing numbers of new people who will, on the basis of human nature, be possessed with a selfish discontent. Even with the Lord Himself on the throne, they will feel that things could be better if they themselves were in control. Multitudes will be redeemed by faith in the Savior-King through the witnessing of faithful Jews — not because His hand is iron and compelling, but because they love and accept Him as Savior and Lord.

It must not be overlooked that conditions will be totally reversed during the Millennium in so far as evangelism is concerned. For the interval of the church age, it has been the Gentiles who were commissioned to lead the world to Christ. To be sure, Jesus' Great Commission was given to His disciples, all of whom were Jews, but the task soon became the responsibility of the Gentiles since the Jews gradually rebelled against the new faith. Granted, not nearly enough has been done to convert the chosen people, but the initiative which we have seen has been taken by Gentile Christians. In the Millennium, it will be the Jews, converted during the seven years of tribulation, who will evangelize the nations. And they will be widely successful. One of the prophets, to whom we have made regular reference, foresees it like this:

> In those days ten men from the nations of every tongue shall take hold of the robe of a Jew, saying, Let us go with you, for we have heard that God is with you.
> Zechariah 8:23 RSV

Isaiah just as excitedly pictures the future glory of Zion and the spread of the righteousness of the Kingdom when he writes,

> And nations shall come to your light,
> and kings to the brightness of your rising.
> Lift up your eyes round about, and see;
> they all gather together, they come to you;
> your sons shall come from far,
> and your daughters shall be carried in the arms.
>
> Isaiah 60:3-4 RSV

> . . .They shall declare my glory among the nations.
>
> Isaiah 66:19 RSV

Nonetheless, in spite of the evangelistic success of the Jews, many will not give glory to the King of their own volition. Their obedience will be given because He is strong and an overthrow of His righteous government is impossible. This, of course, accounts for the fact that the Millennial reign is to be invincible. No force on earth can compare with the power of the God of creation.

## Satan's Last Stand

Lest unredeemed men and women in the millennial period be able to say that they had no chance to express their true wills, a brief time will be arranged at the close of the thousand year period for just such personal expression. Although the people shall have lived under a perfectly just and righteous system of government, there are many who will revolt against the King at that time. Their cry will still be, "We will not have this man to rule over us." Thus, the depravity of human nature is going to be seen stripped bare of any pretense when man proudly challenges the gracious rule of the Lord Himself, even when he has witnessed the benefits of His love enjoyed by all. Furthermore, it will be plain for all to see that man's nature can never be changed with anything less than an inner transformation of heart motive by the acceptance of Christ as Lord and Savior.

Giving them the opportunity to choose between Himself and His sworn enemy, God will release Satan from the pit where he has been bound throughout the Millennium. John tells us the way it will happen.

> When the thousand years end, Satan will be let out of his prison. He will go out to deceive the nations of the world and gather them together, with Gog and Magog, for battle – a mighty host, numberless as sand along the shore. They will go up across the broad plain of the earth and surround God's people and the beloved city of Jerusalem on every side.
>
> Revelation 20:7-9 LB

At the time of the exodus of the devil from his pit of confinement, great hordes of people who have never been tempted before, will be seduced into a participation in an uprising against the King on David's throne. These people will come from all over the earth, not just from the old northern kingdom of Gog which was devastated by God in its invasion of Israel early in the last prophetic week. The reference here to Gog and Magog indicates that the objective of the people will be the same, but the result will be a repeat performance of what happened to Russia – still remembered by some after a thousand years! Gog and Magog, at that time, will have become a byword of defeat.

The Attack is to be made directly on "the beloved city of Jerusalem." Again, all the power of evil is said to be hurled against the one spot on earth where righteousness and truth is concentrated. To conquer that city would be to overthrow David's throne, capture the King, and win in the age-old conflict between God and Lucifer. Every citizen of the millennial era is to be given the choice to accept Christ and live forever in the eternal state, or to choose Satan's way and spend eternity in hell. The fact that many will choose to cast their lot with the Evil One will prove once and for all that not even the most perfect conditions and the most excellent environment of a whole millennium will suffice to change man's heart. Nothing can ever alter the nature of man except an inner relationship with the living Christ by saving faith in His person and work.

After a thousand years, the Antichrist and the false prophet are still seen in "the lake of fire" awaiting the arrival of the next occupant. Hell is everlasting retribution and there is no escape from it ever! The fire of heaven, like that which fell on Sodom, will consume the armies of Satan as they come against Jerusalem. Then God shall deal with the devil in ultimate judgment. He will "be thrown into the Lake of Fire burning with sulphur where the Creature and the False Prophet are, and they will be tormented day and night forever and ever" (Revelation 20:10 LB). At last the Scourge of all time will be everlastingly punished. His cause will be irremediably lost. And the righteous will stand at the threshold of everlasting joy and peace.

One word should be said at this point about the wicked angels, the demonic spirits who have served Satan so well in his influence and possession of men's minds and bodies. Of these fallen angels Jude writes, "The angels that did not keep their own position but left their proper dwelling have been kept by him in eternal chains in the nether gloom until the judgment of the great day" (Jude 6 RSV). Simon Peter makes mention of this same pit-dwelling of the wicked angels until the judgment (2 Peter 2:4). And when Jesus gives His discourse on the future of the nations, He states that this "eternal fire" has been "prepared for the devil and his angels" (Matthew 25:41 RSV). Thus, it is rather clear that the Beast and false prophet will be the first to suffer the torments of hell, the devil and his demonic company to follow after one thousand years. This will be the beginning of the divine solution to the problem of pollution since all contamination on the earth has its source in the work of Satan.

## Before the Supreme Court at Last

One thing remains to be done after the "devil and his angels" are cast into hell. It is commonly known as the Great White Throne Judgment. The definitive title comes from the Apocalypse itself: "Then I saw a great white throne and him who sat upon it; from his presence earth and sky fled away, and no place was found for them" (Revelation 20:11 RSV). This is not "the judgment seat of Christ" where the saints received their rewards. Neither is this "the judgment of the nations" at the end of the great tribulation. This is the *final judgment* upon the wicked dead from the beginning of the human race until the end of the Millennium. Already we have discussed the first resurrection. The second resurrection takes place a thousand years after the first. It is a resurrection unto eternal death. Of this event John writes,

> The rest of the dead [men and women who are left behind at the translation of the Church] did not come to life until the thousand years were ended . . . Blessed and holy are those who have part in the first resurrection. The second death has no power over them. . . . And I saw the dead, great and small, standing before the throne, and books were opened. Another book was opened, which is the book of life. The dead were judged according to what they had done as recorded in the books. The sea gave up the dead that were in it, and death and Hades gave up the dead that were in them, and each person was judged according to what he had done. Then death and Hades were thrown into the lake of fire. The lake of fire is the second death. If anyone's name was not found written in the book of life, he was thrown into the lake of fire.
>
> Revelation 20:5, 6, 12-14 LB

Jesus warned the people that "the hour is coming when all who are in the tombs will hear his voice and come forth, those who have done good, to the resurrection of life, and those who have done evil, to the resurrection of judgment" (John 5:28-28 ). Paul is certain ". . . that there will be a resurrection of both the just and the unjust" (Acts 24:15). The presence of the "book of life" at this final judgment is conclusive proof that the dead called forth from the grave (whether in the earth or in the sea) are lost due to their failure to accept Christ as Savior. *Hades*, where they had been awaiting the time of the judgment, was its own guarantee of lostness. The use of "the books" infers that the *levels* of punishment are determined on the basis of works. If there are varied rewards in heaven, then surely there must be varied degrees of punishment in hell.

At this juncture in the program of divine events, hell will be over-populated! With the harvest of the wicked of all the ages, hell is said to be a place where "there shall be weeping and gnashing of teeth" (Matthew 8:12; 22:13; 24:51; 25:30; Luke 13:28). Such a scenario suggests deplorable conditions of unbearable proximity. And while hell becomes over-populated (that fate is a part of the punishment), the population problem on the earth will be solved at last.

## Cleansing the Land

Long ago, the princely prophet looked forward to a time when the world would be purified of everything which has interfered with the beauty, peace, and harmony designed by the Creator. He heard God saying,

> For behold, I create new heavens
> and a new earth;
> and the former things shall not
> be remembered
> or come into mind.

Isaiah 65:17 RSV

John gives us a radiant picture of what that new realm will be like (Revelation 21:1-22:5). But the one New Testament penman who explains how it will happen is Saint Peter.

> The day of the Lord is surely coming, as unexpectedly as a thief, and then the heavens will pass away with a terrible noise and the heavenly bodies will disappear in fire, and the earth and everything on it will be burned up. . . . You should look forward to that day and hurry it along – the day when God will set the heavens on fire, and the heavenly bodies will melt and disappear in flames. But we are looking forward to God's promise of new heavens and a new earth afterwards, where there will be only goodness.
>
> 2 Peter 3:10, 12, 13 LB

By these words we are not to assume that Peter means annihilation. Not one bit of matter which God has made will ever be done away. The conflagration which is here depicted will change the form of matter, but not annihilate it. Nothing God has ever made will be deprived of existence. It may disappear from the natural eye, be transformed into gas or energy, but it does not cease to be. Man himself lives forever somewhere in some changed condition. Hell does not do away with man any more than heaven puts an end to him. Likewise, the universe was made by God and nothing good will be annihilated. But it will be changed from the global matter which we now know into a new form of habitable existence. Certainly, "the new heavens and the new earth" will be conducive to the kind of bodies the saints of God will receive in the world to come.

If one is concerned about the state of the people of God during this terrible holocaust, let it be noted that God protected the three Hebrew children from the fiery blast even within the framework of Nebuchadnezzar! If He could do it then, He can do it again.  Do not overlook the fact that there is something indestructible about righteousness.  It lives on through the fire.

Plainly, the Scriptures teach us that everything that defiles or pollutes will be burnt out of the universe.  Sin's contamination will be gone forever.  The pollutants which have alarmed us of late are destined for the divine fire.  One day the heavens are going to be cleared of all which now makes the atmosphere a risk to breathe.  The waters will be purified and life will abound within them.  With all the contaminants of the soil gone, the earth will be totally free of its curse and man will live in harmony with it as did Adam before his sin.  God hates pollution.  He has promised to deal with it.  And He will!  In the next chapter, we shall see some of the renovated splendor which may be expected in the life that shall one day become a blessed reality to the people of the Lord.

# Chapter 12

# God's Solution To The World's Blight

## Restoration of the Earth Itself

From the creation of "the heavens and the earth" (Genesis 1:1) to the creation of "a new heaven and a new earth" (Revelation 21:1), all existence has been restricted to a space-time continuum. Before the universe came into being at the Word of God, there was no space nor was there any time. This is what is called *eternity*. Following the conflagration, which will purify the cosmos at the end of the age, all being will return to the ante-creation state. Eternity is going to be spaceless (in the sense of unlimited) and timeless (in the sense of unending). Our present world order has been an interval or parenthesis between these two eternities.

The new earth will have been fully cleansed by the purgating fires of the Creator Himself. Everything will have the distinct look and feel of newness and freshness about it. Assuredly, there will still be points of recognition even as Jesus' resurrection body was identifiable by the disciples. Yet, in the same manner in which those disciples found the Master's appearance splendidly different, so the earth is to be reformed by God.

Those surprises which await us in the world to come are bound to be far more exciting and eternally exhilarating than anyone can describe with his human vocabulary. John has this universal problem in trying to draw word pictures of what he saw in his vision. When he talks about gold streets, pearly gates, gem-studded walls, and inexhaustible light, it is obvious that he is desperately seeking to depict an eternal glory with the best analogies available. We almost sense the apostle's frustration in being unable to find the words which will really convey the unutterable beauty of the new earth.

One of the first observations made by the seer is that "the sea was no more" (Revelation 21:1). The seas have always been symbolic of separation and loneliness. It is the vast bodies of water which divide the continents and people of the earth. When one recalls that John was on an island away from the mainland where was his beloved Ephesus, the feeling of being shut out and alone is greatly heightened. Apparently, the oceans with their pollution are to be no more. Renewed humanity will have nothing to divide man from man. The only source of water will be "the river of the water of life, bright as crystal, flowing from the throne of God and of the Lamb" (22:1 RSV). And it is to be as uncontaminated as is the nature of the God who sits on the throne from which it issues. Like the river which "flowed out of Eden to water the garden" (Genesis 2:10), the heavenly river will bring health and healing to all. "To the thirsty," says the Lord, "I will give water without price from the fountain of the water of life" (Revelation 21:6 RSV).

## Renovation of the Heavenly Sphere

It seems that the new heaven will be without sun, moon, or stars. A connection may be found here between the ancient tendency to worship the celestial hosts (as well as the modern affinity for sun-worship) and the ultimate disappearance of any substitute for the living God. Numbers of prophecies suggest that something is going to happen to the heavenly luminaries in the coming world. Joel says that in the latter days "the sun and the moon shall be dark, and the stars shall withdraw their shining" (Joel 2:10; 3:15). In his prophecy regarding the Messianic Kingdom and the troublous days which accompany it (which word Peter insists was partially fulfilled at Pentecost — Acts 2:17-

21), Joel is specific: "The sun shall be turned to darkness, and the moon into blood, before the great and terrible day of the Lord come" (Joel 2:31).

Our Lord speaks of the same fate for the shining hosts of heaven in His warning related to the *parousia* of the Son of man: "After the tribulation of those days, the sun will be darkened, and the moon will not give its light, and the stars will fall from heaven, and the powers of the heavens will be shaken" (Matthew 24:29; cf. Mark 13:24; Luke 23:45). In the beginning of the created order, God dispelled the darkness of the formless deep through an act by which the transcendent Creator became imminent in His creation. "Let there be light," said God, "and there was light. And God saw that the light was good; and God separated the light from the darkness" (Genesis 1:3-4 RSV). Clearly, we see that there was light long before the appearance of the "lights in the firmament of the heavens" (1:14 RSV). The sun, moon, and stars were not formed until the fourth day while the light itself was the result of God's first day of creation. The celestial lights are nothing more than concentrations of the light in circumscribed areas. In each instance, they are only reflective of the divine light which is the imminent God of all.

In view of this clear-cut observation, it is not hard to conceive of a world in which the sun, moon, and stars have been removed without resulting in darkness! Writing in his first epistle, John says, "God is light and in him is no darkness at all" (1 John 1:5). Malachi promised that the day would come when "the sun of righteousness *shall* rise with healing in his wings" (Malachi 4:2). And when Jesus, the Son of God who is the source of all light, came into the world, He declared, "I am the light of the world" (John 8:12; 9:5). The Apocalypse informs us that "the city has no need of the sun or moon to shine upon it, for the glory of God is its light, and its lamp is the Lamb" (Revelation 21:23; cf. 22:5 RSV). We are further told that those who surround the throne, having come out of great tribulation, shall dwell where "the sun shall not strike them, nor any scorching heat" (7:16 RSV). The Trinity, source of ineffable light, will provide all the light needed in the heavenly state.

Of additional insight is the story of Jesus' transfiguration where ". . . his face shone like the sun, and his garments became white as light" (Matthew 17:2 RSV). This was a foretaste of what we may anticipate in the world to come. In the center of the vision given to John, stood one whose "face was like the sun shining in full strength" (Revelation 1:16; cf. 10:1 RSV). It was this same light which struck Saul of Tarsus with temporary blindness (Acts 9:3, 8, 9) and was later described by him as ". . . a light from heaven, brighter than the sun, shining round me . . ." (Acts 26:13 RSV). Thus, we perceive that no luminous bodies will be needed to reflect the light of God where He is so fully present. The only possible reflection of divine brightness in heaven will be the people themselves who, Jesus says, "will shine like the sun in the kingdom of their Father" (Matthew 13:43 RSV).

## A New City for the Old Ones

Talk about urban renewal! If the transformation brought to metropolitan slum areas, by man's skill at modernizing his environment, is thought to be a spectacular achievement, what must the righteous have yet to see in the New Jerusalem! On earth, crews of workmen set themselves to the task of clearing away the downtown eyesores and replacing them with high-rise offices. In the process, vermin-infested tenements are obliterated and the cesspools of disease and pollution are done away. God must have something of the same thing in mind in His plans for the New Jerusalem, plans which are shared with us in the book of Revelation. "Nothing unclean shall enter it, nor anyone who practices abomination or falsehood, but only those who are written in the Lamb's book of life" (Revelation 21:27 RSV) and "there shall no more be anything accursed" (Revelation 22:3 RSV). In the initial section of this chapter, we looked at the pure river flowing from the midst of this city. Beside that river there is to be "the tree of life with its twelve kinds of fruit, yielding its fruit each month; and the leaves of the tree are for the healing of the nations" (22:2 RSV). Obviously, the fruit of this tree, whose roots draw from the pure water of life in the river, are health-giving like that which grew on the tree of life in the Garden of Eden (Genesis 2:9). The fruit on that tree would have made man live forever, but Adam chose instead to eat from the forbidden tree of the knowledge of good and evil. For that sin, he was driven from the garden and debarred from the tree of life (Genesis 3:22-24). Someday, in the heavenly world, God's redeemed children will be permitted access to that old life-giving tree and we shall live forever!

The account states that the renovated city of God was seen "coming down . . . out of heaven prepared as a bride adorned for her husband" (Revelation 21:2). The New Jerusalem is to be understood, therefore, as both a city and a people. It is likely that this city will be suspended in the air above the land of Palestine during the Millennium and, at its end, will descend to the renewed earth. Another reference is made to the Bride as the holy city in verse nine of this same chapter. Since the Bride is always to be equated in Scripture with the Church, it is likely that this is where the translated Church of Christ will dwell during the millennial reign. This explains how glorified bodies (in the exalted city above the earth) and mortal bodies (on the earth) can live together for the thousand years of peace. The city is seen as something "coming down," however, which means that its final position will be on the earth. This will take place after the burning holocaust which purifies the world at the genesis of the coming eternal state. While the city is suspended above the earth, the saints who have had part in the first resurrection will probably share with the Bride. This seems to be borne out by John's seeing twelve gates inscribed with the names of the Jewish tribes and twelve foundation stones inscribed with the names of the apostles.

Can we begin to conceive the breathtaking beauty of a city which has streets of transparent gold and whose walls are everywhere plastered with precious gems? With the light of God sparkling on each jeweled prism and producing a kaleidoscope of brilliant light, heaven must be fantastic beyond our loftiest expectation. "By its light shall the nations [peoples] walk . . ." (Revelation 21:24 RSV). And no wonder! From this city, which will be the center of the heavenly world, the glorified sons of God will have access to all the earth and the farthest reaches of the spaceless universe. Jesus may have had this in mind when He said, "In my Father's house are many rooms . . ." (John 14:2 RSV). Indeed, the Father's house is vaster by far than our telescopes suggest.

### New People for a New World

"Behold, the dwelling of God is with men. He will dwell with them and they shall be his people, and God himself will be with them" (Revelation 21:3 RSV). From the beginning of man's existence, the Lord God has been creating a people for Himself. After all the centuries and millennia of discipline, chastisement, and punishment – at last, His plan will be completed. The relationship will be what man has dreamed about and sought after through all his days: "I will be his God and he shall be my son" (21:7). That is the divine promise to him who overcomes in the struggle against evil. Of course, the victory itself belongs to Christ whose Spirit wins for him who trusts in His atoning work on the cross.

To worship and glorify God, who has redeemed us, will fill our days with joy and gladness. We "shall see his face, and his name shall be on [our] foreheads" (22:4 RSV). Oh, the joy of seeing Him whom our hearts have felt and our minds have followed! Man's deepest desire is to see God. To look upon the face of His redeeming Son, who has saved us from death and hell, will be to know the satisfaction of our eternal aspirations.

No more will the wicked shatter the blessedness of His people. No more will Satan interfere. No more will man struggle against the curses of our modern world – scourges like war, pollution, and starvation. No more will the people of God suffer the indignities of both religious and political corruption which swirl like a gushing cesspool across the planet. "The cowardly, the unbelieving, the vile, the murderers, the sexually immoral, those who practice magic arts, the idolater and all liars – their place will be in the fiery lake of burning sulphur" (21:8 NIV). Emphasizing the same point of exclusion of everyone and everything which would contaminate the new world, John says, "Outside the city are those who have strayed away from God, and the sorcerers, and the immoral and murderers, and idolaters, and all who love to lie, and do so" (22:15 LB). Emphatically, the impression given by the prophecy of John is that the heavenly world will be a prepared place for a prepared people.

## Not Possible to Imagine

No one will die in heaven. "The last enemy that shall be destroyed is death" (1 Corinthians 15:26). And in that life for which all creation groans ". . . death shall be no more" (21:4 RSV). The child of God will be immortal in his glorified body, a body like unto that of Jesus following the Resurrection. The entire verse from which the above quote is taken includes more than death in its list of missing things.

> He will wipe away every tear from their eyes. There will be no more death or mourning or crying or pain, for the old order of things has passed away.
>
> Revelation 21:4 NIV

These words clarify more than at first meets the eye. If there are no tears or pain, then everything which has caused man trouble in his earthly pilgrimage will be missing. This does not imply stagnation in a sterile climate. Far from it. What it does imply is that the righteous will finally be able to be and do that which God originally intended for them. There will be no deterrents to hinder their growth and loving service. The hindrances will have been conquered and rendered inoperative and impotent as we enter through the gates of the city.

Contrary to the scholarly opinions of many within the Church today, God has chosen to reveal a great part of His plan for the world. The future is not shrouded in mystery for him who will arduously search the Scriptures. The Bible – both Old and New Testaments – is God's message to man. For too long we have either ignored it or mutilated it with our irreverent criticisms. It is time that we allow the Scriptures to speak to us in their clear, powerful, divine voice. Any man can understand enough prophecy not to be caught by surprise when the Lord comes for His Church. The world events which are taking place all around us in these days are all a part of the divine plan. This is not to say that God causes the deplorable events which transpire around us, but He permits them because He knows in advance that this is the way the human race is going. His plan is a correction of what the divine mind has always known would happen. We are foolish beyond words to describe, if we neglect the prophetic calendar and guidebook which can lead us out of a world destined for judgment.

While God has chosen to reveal much of His plan for the winding up of this present world order, He has told us very little about the eternal dimension which we have been discussing in this chapter. That is His secret which He is keeping as a surprise for His own. What little we have been permitted to see has only whetted our appetites for more. Therefore, we have begun the journey to "Canaan's fair and happy land" and some of us are well on our way. The farther along the way we get, the more excited we become. But let us be patient, "Looking for that blessed hope . . ." (Titus 2:13) until the promise of God is fulfilled in us on the hills of that eternal city!

# Chapter 13

# The Clock Is Running Down

*A Historical Overview*

Zephaniah warned the Israelites in the seventh century before Christ that the Chaldeans were coming. No one would believe it. But they came anyway and the people were carried into captivity. Jesus warned the Israelites that their nation would be overrun and the Temple destrcyed within a generation. Nobody believed it. But the Romans came and the last vestige of a nation destined to be God's light to the world was erased from the scene. The United States has been the world's leading power for longer than some of us can remember. Voices are now warning us that the end of our glory is drawing near, that "the great democracy" is about to end. But does anyone believe it? Only a scattered handful. Every poll taken indicates that the masses believe that the future for America can only get better. Usually, such persons are thinking in terms of economy alone. Even the economic prognosis is not assured. Before the day of America's grandeur, it was England who stood on top of the world. And prior to England, it was France, Spain, Rome, Greece, Babylon, and Egypt. Every time there were seers to predict what was soon to happen, but in no case did enough people believe it to alter the destiny of an empire.

In the *Decline and Fall of the Roman Empire*, Gibbon gives several reasons for the deterioration and collapse of Rome. The people played loose with morals to the point of desecrating the family and nearly destroying the home. When the family goes, the nation goes, too. Taxes were exorbitant and unwisely used to provide support and entertainment for the masses, many of whom did not contribute their share. Practically all the populace was obsessed with an insatiable thirst for pleasure. Sports were more important than employment or faith. A massive system of weaponry was created and continuously added to under the certainty of a false security. All the while there was an inner decay at the heart of the empire – a rejection of responsibility on the part of the citizens themselves. What was probably worst of all, religion – pagan as it may have been –was neglected and materialism smothered almost every trace of awe and reverence for the supernatural.

History reveals that, while some empires have gone down in battle and others have been taken without a shot, the general pattern has been the same. One of the above criteria always characterizes a fallen people. Usually there is a combination of several or all of them. Anyone can easily see that the United States fits the total description to perfection. But the most telling observation of our modern time is that, for the first time, one or more of these characteristics can be found in every nation on the face of the earth. In fact, the whole world in general is accurately pictured in Gibbon's five points of decline in the Roman Empire. This, in itself, is one good reason to believe, from a historical analysis alone, that the human race as a whole is nearing its demise.

## Interest in Biblical Prophecy Mounts

Every generation has a few persons concerned enough with prophecy to speak out on the subject. Occasionally, some enthusiastic seer will try to pinpoint the exact date of the end of the world. Not since the days of the New Testament Church, however, has there been as much worldwide interest in biblical prophecy as in recent times. Quite suddenly, the Holy Spirit seems to be removing the scales from our eyes and people everywhere, especially young people, are asking for illumination on the subject of "last things." Even people who have not been too involved in the religious activity of their home church are beginning to get excited about the prospects for the consummation of the ages inherent in our time. When Michael the Archangel concluded his instructions to Daniel relating to the end of the world, he specifically described our own age as the time when the prophecies would be understood.

But Daniel, keep this prophecy a secret; seal it up so that it will not be understood until the end times, when travel and education shall be vastly increased!

Daniel 12:4 LB

Young people have become strangely knowledgeable in biblical prophecy. It has happened almost spontaneously and with very little instruction. It is as if the Spirit had broken open His sealed mysteries and poured them into the hearts and minds of millions of youthful witnesses. Scientists, educators, philosophers, business men, professional people, and housewives are sharing the prophetic word. Once in a while a clergyman is found who will risk a few words on the subject! Back in the seventeenth century, Isaac Newton said, "About the Time of the End, a body of men will be raised up who will turn to the Prophecies, and insist upon their literal interpretations, in the midst of much clamor and opposition." That time is now. The prophets are crying out, "Thus saith the Lord!" And, as should be expected, the ridicule of both religious and non-religious people and institutions is widespread. Daniel's heavenly visitor had a sobering word to say about this rebel attitude.

Go now, Daniel, for what I have said is not to be understood until the time of the end. Many shall be purified by great trials and persecutions. But the wicked shall continue in their wickedness, and none of them will understand. Only those who are willing to learn will know what it means.

Daniel 12:4 LB

Considering the incontestable evidence that every prophecy relating to the birth of Christ, the first Advent of the Messiah, was fulfilled to the letter, it would be a bit unexplainable if we were to doubt the certainty of literal fulfillment for those having to do with His return. And it would also be strange for disciples of Christ to question the integrity of Jesus or the veracity of His words about the kind of conditions which will prevail on the earth immediately before His Second Advent. He has never been found wrong. Lately, many of His prophetic words are coming true in precise detail as He said they would.

Scarcely any generation since the days of Christ's earthly ministry has been without some signs of the end. Ours, however, has seen more fulfilled prophecies in a shorter period of time than any previous generation. *This makes our time different from all previous periods of history.* Those who argue that there have always been signs, and prophets to call attention to them, do not seriously consider the rapid multiplication of those signs in our day. To fail to make that vitally significant observation is tragic. Not a single day passes without the observers of world events calling our attention to developments which cannot be understood apart from prophecy.

### Widespread Concern about Preparation

When a man has a premonition that he is going to die, he almost always acts in a certain way. His demeanor will become deeply serious and, with the strength and time he has left, a man inevitably tries to get his affairs in shape and his house in order. We are seeing exactly this kind of serious concentration and hurried effort by the nations today. There is a growing premonition that civilization is in its last hours. And instead of turning to God and relaxing in His divine providence, we intensify our human drive to set straight the house of the world. A kind of death struggle is upon the nations as a rebel race gives one last push to building a perfect kingdom of man. At the bottom of our struggle is an international awareness that we have dug our own grave and that the shroud is laid out.

Everything on the world scene is shaping up just as the Bible says it will at the end. Man is doing what is natural in the approach of global death. God has told us that certain things will happen as the world's breath grows short. In a quick recap of what has been said in foregoing pages, let us look at some of the most obvious signs of the end of the age as the Word of God portrays it.

We have seen the restoration of the Jewish people in their own land by act of the United Nations. The one unfulfilled prophecy, which annulled all talk of the coming of Christ and the winding up of our world order in the past, was the promise of Israel's return to Palestine. That had to take place before the end could come. And it did happen in 1948. Furthermore, the Jews were promised control of the holy city again. For the first time since the days of Christ, the city of Jerusalem was recaptured in 1967. Our generation has seen history made and prophecy realized in an astounding manner. Jesus clearly affirmed that the Jews would be in Palestine and Jerusalem when He returns. He also stated that "this generation [the generation living when the Jewish nation is restored] will not pass away till all these things take place" (Matthew 24:34; Mark 13:30; Luke 21:32 ). The generation which has seen these things transpire is ours!

Scripture indicates that the Temple of the Jews will be rebuilt on Mount Zion before the *parousia* (2 Thessalonians 2; Matthew 24:15, 16). As yet, that Temple is not constructed, but plans are underway to erect the edifice as soon as possible. Since such a feat could be on its way at any moment, and since the Church will be translated before its construction by Antichrist, the coming of Christ for His Bride could happen tonight!

Ezekiel is not at all cryptic when he tells us that Russia and her confederates will invade Israel. Nor are we left in the dark as to what to expect from the Arabic world including both the African Arabs (Libya) and the Black Africans (Ethiopia). The relationship between Russia and the Arab world today is exactly what we should expect if the end is near. And the mighty hosts of China, now in readiness to cross the Euphrates River and share in the final war, is an integral part of the picture. No one can possibly miss the significance of the European Union which has laid the groundwork out of which the revived Roman Empire shall rise and from which will issue the Antichrist.

All over the world the cry is raised, "Peace! Peace!" The Church has joined in the religious-sounding demands for a world without war even though Jesus told us it would never happen. Masses of people display the crow's foot as their expression of resistance to war. Nevertheless, in the midst of all the talk about world peace, the nations continue to badger one another and prepare for the war of all wars which everyone subconsciously knows to be on the way. Never before have men been more interested in peace and less able to achieve it than right now.

Added to this should be a word about mankind's rabid interest in the heavens. Jesus said that there would be signs in the sun and other heavenly bodies. While His specific reference was to the change that will take place in these luminaries themselves, it is of importance to note that man is more interested in outer space with its distant planets and stars today than ever before. Our space program grows out of an insatiable desire to know more about the far-away bodies of light in the heavens. And in conjunction with this scientific probe is the revival of pagan star-worship by millions of duped people who live on the authority of astrological prognosticators. Our obsession with the sun, moon, and stars keeps us looking up. That may be a form of preparation for our seeing the upheaval in the heavens and the appearing of Christ in the clouds of judgment.

## Nothing Will Clean Up Our Mess

Famine stalks the earth and reaps untold numbers of men, women, and children. Lean, gaunt bodies, with huge eyes staring out at us in helplessness, greet us in the daily newspapers and on television. Earthquakes occur lately with more frequency and do more damage to life and property than ever before. Seismologists are predicting that the problem is getting worse, that we are sitting on a keg of dynamite which can be ignited at any moment. Violence in the streets has become an international concern. People are afraid to walk the streets alone in our major cities in broad daylight. Racial tension is at an all- time high even though blacks and whites keep smiling as though the whole thing were under control. Authority in government, education, religion, and the home is rejected. Every individual does as he pleases and the whole world suffers. The "bewilderment" of which the Lord spoke (Luke 21:25) is all around us.

These are the times when men "bring upon themselves quick destruction" (2 Peter 2:1). An example of this is found in what was experienced by the people of Hiroshima and has been feared by every man alive since that sad day. But we have many ways of bringing quick death to ourselves and others. Our drug epidemic is leaving tragedy in its wake. Wild and senseless abandonment to sex and perversion is only symptomatic of our bent toward self-destruction. Experimentation with evil powers, demonic forces, astrology, and satanic cultism bring with it insanity and uncontrollable fear.

Religious institutions are dying everywhere. The organized church is in serious trouble, so much so that large groups have decided to pool their dwindling forces in a united conglomerate. Maybe the image of bigness and oneness and cooperation will give them a few more days of grace. All of it is being promoted under the ruse of becoming the Church of Christ in unity of purpose and spirit. Regardless as to what we hear in glowing pronouncements of positive value in the movement, what we see does not bear out the truth of the praises sounded by the uniting strategists. The faith of the apostles is so emasculated of its content and power that there is nothing left but a religious shell. If the living gospel of Jesus Christ were to be put in that brittle shell, it would literally explode. No one pays much attention anymore to the theologically liberal organized church, its seminars, or its official declarations. Why should he? There is nothing really distinctive about such an organized church today except in those rare instances where a local congregation has been "turned on" by the Holy Spirit. The desiccated shell of uniting organizations has served the cause of Satan well in paving the way for the apostate institution of the tribulation and its false prophet.

## Signs of Encouragement

Right in the middle of the wickedness, pride, and apostasy of these days, the Holy Spirit is doing a great work. The laity is bypassing the normal busyness of the church and discovering the power of a Spirit-filled life. Thousands of lay people from nearly all doctrinal strains are teaming up in mission outside the walls of their own parish. Campus organizations continue to spring up to witness to college students. Prayer groups of teens are forming in high schools. In-depth Bible study cells are being arranged by hungry men and women who have not been fed from the Word in their local churches. A cadre of resistance to the teaching of evolution in our schools is growing. And the refusal to accept the legislation prohibiting the posting of the Ten Commandments in our schools and government buildings without a fight is a refreshing sign. The transformation taking place in the lives of individuals, who have come into a saving relationship with Jesus Christ, is loudly pronounced by the *shekinah* (presence of God) on their countenances.

The name of Jesus is being seen everywhere as though it belongs in all areas of man's culture. And , indeed, it does. Certainly, there is a chance that His worthy name may be prostituted in some instances by being associated with evil surroundings. But He who was unafraid of being contaminated by associating with sinners is not at all alarmed in finding His name in strange and even wicked places. On the contrary! Where else would we expect to find Him if He were here in the flesh?

The whole world is having a phenomenal opportunity to become acquainted with Jesus Christ. No one can plead ignorance any longer. Christ is all about us without disguise. His Holy Spirit is working in the open and lives are being touched in every city and hamlet of the world. Mass communication media are getting involved in the work of the Lord — often without knowing it. The entire spiritual aura prevailing in our world of sham and pretense is a sure sign that God is "pouring out His Spirit upon all flesh" (see Joel 2:28 and Acts 2:17).

As this Spirit confronts the world, not every person will be saved. There is no warrant in the Scriptures for believing that such will ever happen. Some are being redeemed and made a part of that Bride for whom our Lord is soon to come. But multitudes are becoming adamant against this "new thing" which the Lord is doing and they are resisting the Spirit. Often these people are staid members of the institutional church and regular attenders at its services of worship. Believers are becoming bolder to witness and a

polarization is developing that will divide the world into two
distinct camps – the Bride and the rejected.

Jesus said, "I came to cast fire on the earth . . . Do you
think that I have come to give peace . . .? No, I tell you, but
rather division" (Luke 12:49, 51 RSV). By that our Lord
acknowledged that His purpose in the world now is
polarization. When men experience the fire of God as did
Pascal, there will be both an honoring of their witness and a
persecution of themselves. We should expect a time of
persecution soon in which Christian witnesses will become
Christian martyrs.

While the Spirit of God is moving in the world and many
are coming to know Christ, there is little reason to believe
that we are on the verge of a great revival. Our Savior
suggested that He might find a scarcity of faith on the earth
when He returns (Luke 18:8). The description which He gives
of the end-times as being like the days of Noah would not
imply a great revival. There are multitudes who are coming
to new life in the Spirit even after having given up on religion
as they have seen it. And, by the same token, many who are
falling away from the Lord are so proud of their professed
religion that they refuse to bow before the atoning Savior.

These are great and terrible days to be alive. They are
both exciting and fearful – exciting because the Lord is due
to come at any moment – fearful because so many are not
ready to enter in with Him to the marriage supper of the
Lamb. To the people who continue to ignore the mighty
penetration of the Spirit in these latter days, we must carry
the dual message of impending judgment or joyous
deliverance. To those who are watching for His appearing,
we must offer words of encouragement and assurance. And
to Him who will one day rend the eastern sky with a shout,
we must say,

# "Come, Lord Jesus!"

# ADDENDUM

# ADDITIONAL THOUGHTS
# ON PROPHECY

Incredibly amazing! No other words can describe the neglect of biblical prophecy which characterizes the world church as it moves into the third millennium of its existence. It is probably safe to suggest that ninety percent of the people who attend Sunday school and church services never hear a lesson or a sermon on prophecy. Yet, more than twenty-five percent of the bible is devoted to this neglected theme. In fact, the thread which runs throughout the entire Bible from Genesis to Revelation is the kingdom of God. It is the one over-riding concept. The tragedy lies in the fact that this central theme cannot be understood apart from a thorough understanding of prophecy. The kingdom of God is proleptic, that is, it is realized in the birth of Jesus Christ and yet anticipated in its fullness when He returns to the earth at the end of the age. Jesus clearly taught this fundamental truth in the model prayer when the disciples were led to pray, "Thy kingdom come, Thy will be done, on earth as it is in heaven." While the kingdom has dawned in Jesus Christ, its full burst of divine power and glory is yet future at which time the promise in the bud becomes the fulfillment of the rose.

It was in the early days of the fourth century that Christianity suffered its first devastating blow. To be sure, the first three hundred years were difficult as the church's greatest spirits suffered and died at the hands of a hostile world government. But the blood of the martyrs was the seed of the church.

Then came the Serbian warrior, later to be remembered as

Constantine the Great, who relaxed the persecution and encouraged everyone to be Christian. While every battle-scarred believer breathed a sigh of relief, the coming years proved the favoritism shown the church to be the worst thing which could have happened. Being a Christian became the respectable thing to do. The masses joined the church and the church began to die. When the world moved into the church, the church became like the world. And the compromise which began during the reign of Constantine continues until this day.

Within seventeen years following the death of Constantine, a boy was born in North Africa, who was to become bishop of Hippo. His name was Aurelius Augustine. At the age of thirty-three, weary with his intellectual pursuits which had left him empty and confused, he was genuinely converted to Christ and baptized by Bishop Ambrose of Milan. The church will always be indebted to Augustine for his defense of the faith against the Manichaeans, the Donatists, and the Palagians, but every saint of God has his weaknesses. And Augustine's was his introduction of a new method of interpreting scripture which was quickly adopted by the already weakened ranks of Christendom. The written word of God, which had thus far been understood in a literal manner, would henceforth be interpreted spiritually. Origin had already played with an allegorical system of explaining the Bible - resultant in part from his teaching of Greek philosophy - but Augustine carried it much further. Scripture had to conform to the teachings of the institutional church which left the door open to arbitrary fancy. The views of Tertullian and Irenaeus were rejected by this new school of thought at Alexandria and the literal understanding of the scriptures espoused by the apostles was soon forgotten. Thus, the kingdom of God ceased to be seen as a literal reign by Christ from Jerusalem and the church became the "new Israel". And biblical prophecy was lost. Augustine's "The City of God" replaced the kingdom of Israel and the new Jerusalem.

The fourth century may be looked back upon as one of the sad and tragic periods for biblical truth. It may be said that the second century was a time when apologetics was considered priority. That is not hard to understand when it is remembered that it was during this time that the Christians had to defend their faith against both pagan Rome and the Gnostics. The third and fourth centuries were concerned with the development of theology since many strange ideas were coming into the now favored fellowship. By the fifth century the prevailing concern was with man himself, a time during which the focus shifted from theology to anthropology. As discussion moved into the sixth century, the personal nature of Christ moved to center stage and the debates and fighting among fellow Christians became heated to a boiling point. Nothing really new happened during the following dark ages until the Reformation in the sixteenth century when soteriology, the study of salvation, demanded attention. The great revival of the eighteenth century grew out of this restatement of justification by faith. And this brings us to prophecy or what is referred to as eschatology. It was the eighteenth century which brought the church back to a new look at a neglected truth, a literal approach to prophecy. Certainly much credit must be given to the Plymouth Brethren of England for recalling us to an ancient church formula for interpreting scripture and understanding the theme which runs throughout the bible - the kingdom of God.

Often we hear someone refer to himself as a New Testament Christian. Well, of course, we all are if we believe in Christ. There is no other kind since there were no Christians in the Old Testament. What such a person usually means, however, is that he is not interested in the Old Testament. And that is not just short-sighted; it is tragic. The Old not only gave birth to the New, but the New cannot be understood apart from the Old. Therefore, any study of prophecy worthy of the name must begin with the Old Testament. The key to eschatology is found primarily in the sixth century prophets of Ezekiel and Daniel. Both were in Babylon as a result of the defeat of Judah and the captivity of her people brought about by Nebuchadnezzar. Were it not for Daniel we would be at a loss to explain the words of our Lord (Matthew 24:15-

28) relating to the great tribulation and the blasphemous desecration of the temple as predicted by the one person who knew what the future holds. What is even more obvious is that the book of Revelation would remain a mystery if it were not for the precise visions of the prophet Daniel.

In the second chapter of Daniel (vss. 31-45) is recorded the interpretation of the king's dream which had been left unexplained by the wisest men of the realm. It remained for the prophet of God to tell Nebuchadnezzar both what he had dreamed and what the dream meant. The revelation came to Daniel in a vision which portrayed the course of world empires and their final destruction by Christ who is "the stone cut out of the mountain without hands". The world empires from the sixth century before Christ until the end of the world are symbolized in the dream by an image comprised of four metals: a head of gold=Babylon, a breast and arms of silver=Medo-Persia, a belly and thighs of bronze=Greece, and legs and feet of iron and clay=Rome. This latter kingdom is symbolized by two legs and ten toes, the legs being the division of the world power into the Eastern and Western Roman Empires and the toes being the conglomerate of nations comprising the kingdom of Rome (Daniel 7:20) when the smiting stone returns to put an end to "the time of the Gentiles" (Luke 21:24). According to Daniel, the western division of the Roman Empire, which fell in 476 AD, and the eastern division, which fell in 1453 AD, will be in place again as a world power at the consummation of the world. It will be ultimately replaced by the smiting stone and the kingdom of God (Revelation 16:13-16). Thus, the empires of man will be destroyed because they all rest upon feet which are a mixture of iron and clay. Man's efforts are unstable and temporary. God's kingdom is sure and eternal. Although Gentile world power begins and ends with a great image (Daniel 2:31 and Revelation 13:14-15), it is destined and doomed from the outset.

Daniel lived to see the Babylonian Empire conquered by Darius the Mede (5:31), a fulfillment of the dream of Nebuchadnezzar relating to the second world empire depicted as a "breast and arms of silver" (2:32). However, not until about eighty-five years after the prophets death in 530 B.C. did the Persian Artaxerxes grant Nehemiah the right to rebuild the walls of Jerusalem by royal edict (Nehemiah 2:1-9). This momentous event took place in the twentieth year of Artaxerxes or 444 B.C., a date of paramount significance to which attention will be called later in this document.

Belshazzar, grandson of Nebuchadnezzar and co-regent with his father Nabonidus, was the acting king on the night when Darius conquered the Babylonian Empire (Daniel 5:1-31). And it was during the first year of Belshazzar's rule (about 553 B.C.) that Daniel had his vision of the four beasts (Daniel 7:1-28) which correspond to the four metals in the image earlier featured in the dream of Nebuchadnezzar. Beginning with Babylon, the world power in force at the commencement of Gentile dominance, and ending with Rome, the four beasts represented the whole of world empires until the end of the world. Here the symbolism changes from gold, silver, bronze, and a mixture of iron and clay to the lion (Babylon), the bear (Medo-Persia), the leopard (Greece), and the composite of the three previous beasts having ten horns (Rome). Among the ten horns arises a "little horn" which subdues three of the kings and totally controls the other seven. This is none other than "the prince that shall come" (9:26), the "abomination" (12:11, Matthew 24:15), and the "beast out of the sea" (Revelation 13:1-10). Paul's "man of sin" (2 Thessalonians 2:4-8) is probably a reference to this same person commonly referred to as the Antichrist. The world empire represented by this "little horn" will be the final kingdom in power when Christ returns to put an end to man's pompous attempts to rule the earth without God (Daniel 7:13-23).

Two years after the aforementioned vision in the first year of Belshazzar's rule, Daniel writes, "a vision appeared unto me . . . after that which appeared unto me at the first" (8:1). Before him appeared a ram with two horns . . . . "but one was higher than the other and the higher came up last" (8:3). Gabriel explains later that "the ram which thou sawest, having two horns, these are the

kings of Media and Persia" (8:20). Then Daniel saw a he-goat with
"a notable horn between his eyes" (8:5) and the he-goat broke the
two horns of the ram, putting an end to the Medes and the
Persians. The he-goat "is the king of Greece", and the great horn
that is between his eyes is the first king (8:21) or Alexander the
Great. In the course of time, the great horn was broken as well
and "four stood up for it" (8:22), that is, Macedonia, Syria, Egypt,
and Asia Minor. Antiochus Epiphanes, the Syrian ruler, was the
"little horn" of Daniel (8:9) and became a type of Antichrist in the
second century before Christ when he made the temple desolate
with his sacrifice by offering swine's flesh on its altars and turning
the sacred precincts into a brothel. The final revelation in the
prophet Daniel's vision of the ram and the he-goat was the birth
of the Roman Empire in "a king of fierce countenance" (8:23) who
is struck down by the King of kings (Revelation 19:11-20) called in
the prophet's vision "the Prince of princes" (8:25).

Having considered the clear key to prophecy in the book of
Daniel with its dreams and visions, it is inconceivable that there
should be any further enlightenment. The most impressive
prophetic display, however, is yet to be found in chapter nine,
verses 20-27. Gabriel, an angel, here praises the prophet for his
receptiveness and assures him that he is greatly loved. The
obvious meaning is that God is pleased with him and is about to
entrust him with the most exacting prediction ever given to mortal
man. Seventy weeks are specified as the time which will pass for
Israel from the decree of Artaxerxes in 444 B.C. which permitted
Nehemiah to return to Jerusalem to rebuild the walls, unto the
completion of God's plan for the nation and the anointings of the
Son of David (Jesus Christ) as king. The seventy weeks are what
is called hebdomads or weeks of years, therefore, the metrical
figure of seventy weeks must be multiplied by seven which gives us
490 years.

Sir Isaac Newton (1642-1727) is still considered to have been
the greatest scientist who ever lived. In his *Observations upon the
Prophecies of Daniel and the Apocalypse of St. John*, published in

London in 1733, there is a clarifying footnote on the above reference to Daniel 9:20-27 which reads in part, "The ancient solar years of the eastern nations consisted of 12 months, and every month of 30 days; and hence came the division of a circle into 360 degrees. This year seems to be used by Moses in his history of the Flood, and by John in the Apocalypse, where a time, times and half a time, 42 months and 1260 days, are put equipollent. But in reckoning by many of these years together, an account is to be kept of the odd days which were added to the end of these years. For the Egyptians added five days to the end of this year; and so did the Chaldeans long before the times of Daniel, as appears by the Bera of Nabouassar; and the Persian Magi used the same year of 365 days, until the Empire of the Arabians. The ancient Greeks also used the same solar year of 12 equal months, or 360 days; but every other year added an intercalary month, consisting of 10 and 11 days alternately."

To paraphrase this passage under scrutiny (Daniel 9:24-27) will be helpful. What Gabriel is here saying to the prophet may be stated as follows. There will be 490 years of chastisement for the nation of Israel before your people will turn from sin and the kingdom of righteousness will be inaugurated at a new consecration of the temple. To be specific, from the command to rebuild Jerusalem unto the coming of the Messiah will be 49 years plus 434 years, the streets and walls being rebuilt during difficult times. At the end of 434 years (plus the 49 needed for rebuilding or 483 years) the Messiah will be killed without realizing his kingdom. The forces of another who proclaims himself the king will destroy the city and the temple, the struggle continuing until the end. This king will sign a treaty with the people for seven years, but at the midway point he will break his pledge, stop all sacrifices, and desecrate the temple. At the end of the seven year treaty, this pretending king will be brought to his knees by the Lord.

Using the time period specified from the command to rebuild the walls on March 4, 444 B.C. unto the crucifixion of Christ on March 29, 33 A.D., one calculates the total to be 476 years and

25 days. If we multiply 476 years times 3655.2419 days for each one of those years (including leap year days), the result is 173,855 days. Then we have to add the 25 additional days which brings the total to 173,880 days, the number of days from the decree of Artaxerxes to the crucifixion. But the prophecy indicates that the years would be 483 rather than 476. Remember that Daniel is speaking of prophetic years of 360 days each. When 483 years are multiplied by 360 days it is discovered that the total is 173,880 days. The prophecy is accurate to the very day!

When Christ was crucified on Good Friday of 33 A.D., the prophetic clock stopped and the nation of Israel was temporarily set aside until a later time in history when God would deal finally with the covenant people who rejected their king. In the interval, He would call out a new people who would become the Bride of Christ as Israel had been the wife of God (read the book of Hosea for insight on God's relationship with Israel). The church was born at Pentecost, fifty days after the resurrection, and would become the people whom the Lord would employ to bring salvation to the world. In no way would the church become the new Israel. The God of Abraham will not break this covenant, but will complete His plan for the Hebrew nation at the end of the church age when Christ returns for the Bride. Therefore, the last seven years in Daniel's prophecy will start the prophetic clock again at the exact moment when it stopped in 33 A.D. Rome, the fourth beast in the prophet's vision, will again be in power and the final chastisement and redemption of the chosen people will be accomplished. Those seven years are known as the great tribulation and are vividly portrayed in Revelation 6-19.

Some may ask what reason can be given for seeing a break between the 69 weeks of years and the final one week. Several facts need to be pointed out. To begin, nothing resembling Daniel's description of the last seven years took place during the week of years following the crucifixion. There was no betrayal at the end of three and one half years, and there was no destruction of city or temple. Titus destroyed Jerusalem thirty seven years later in 70 A.D., not during the seven years after the Messiah was killed. Furthermore, it is agreed by Bible students that the sixty-nine weeks of years are to be taken literally and that they begin with Artaxerxes of Persia. Why then should the last week be anything other than a literal seven year period? It should be remembered that Daniel knew nothing about the church. He had never heard it mentioned. There was assuredly no such thing in his day. The entire period from the cross to the tribulation was unrevealed to him and he wrote far more than he understood. That is true of all the authentic prophets. Their message was not their own. It was God's and they recorded only what He told them to write. For this reason, their pronouncements were prefaced with the words, "Thus saith the Lord". All Daniel saw was a break between the sixty-ninth and seventieth weeks. The church would not be a theocracy, a nation ruled by God through priests, as was Israel. Rather it would be a redeemed fellowship in the hearts of which would dwell the Holy Spirit, and there is nothing relating to the sixty-nine weeks or the seventieth which has anything to do with the church. All of it has to do with the nation of Israel.

One thing often overlooked in the New Testament is reference to the church as a "mystery". Jesus had just told the story of the sower and the seed when His disciples asked why He spoke in parables. His reply was, "Because it is given unto you to know the mysteries of the kingdom of heaven, but to them it is not given" (Matthew 13:11). A mystery was previously hidden truth which was now made manifest. Jesus was speaking of the church which neither Daniel nor anyone else understood before the coming of Jesus. In Revelation 17:5 John envisions the harlot religious conglomerate of the tribulation period who disguises herself as the true church with a name, "Mystery, Babylon the Great, the mother of harlots, and abominations of the earth". Paul writes to the Corinthians, "Let a man so account of us, as of the ministers of Christ, and stewards of the mysteries of God" and "We speak the wisdom of God in a mystery, even the hidden wisdom, which God ordained before the ages unto our glory; which none of the princes of this age knew; for had they known it, they would not have crucified the Lord of glory" (1 Corinthians 4:1, 2:7-8). Paul's more elaborate discussion of the church as a mystery is in Ephesians (3:3-6) where he exclaims, "by revelation he made known unto me the mystery . . . . which in other ages was not made known unto the sons of men, as it is now revealed unto his holy apostles and prophets by the Spirit: that the Gentiles should be fellow heirs, and the same body, and partakers of his promise in Christ by the gospel" (read also Ephesians 1:9-10, 6:19, Colossians 1:24-27). John, in his vision from Patmos of the seven churches portrayed as lampstands, hears a voice saying, "the mystery of the seven stars which thou sawest in my right hand, and the seven golden lampstands. The seven stars are the angels of the churches; and the seven lampstands which thou sawest are the seven churches" (Revelation 1:20). And finally, waxing eloquent about life after death for the church of Christ, Paul writes, "Behold, I show you a mystery: we shall not all sleep, but we shall all be changed, in a moment, in the twinkling of an eye, at the last trump; for the trumpet shall sound, and the dead shall be raised incorruptible, and we shall all be changed" (read also 1 Thessalonians 4:13-18). So the break between week 69 and 70 is understandable. It was a mystery and Daniel did not know what he was seeing. God, however, has made it visible unto us.

There was no nation of Israel from 70 A.D. until 1948 when the new state of Israel was reborn. During that period of time there has been a church, the parenthesis between Daniel's sixty-nine weeks and the seventieth. John the Apostle equates Daniel's seventieth week with the end of the world in revelation. The church age will end at the beginning of that final seven years of trouble. And all indications are that we are very close to that concluding moment of history.

> "The true God is a living, intelligent, and powerful
> being. His duration reaches from eternity to eternity; His
> presence from infinity to infinity. He governs all things.
> -Sir Isaac Newton, Principia (Second Edition)

# CONCERNS OFTEN OVERLOOKED

Among the marvels in history must be included the Maya civilization of Central America which thrived from 250 to 900 A.D. Suddenly, after 650 years of a bloody and yet incredibly advanced culture, the people walked away without a word of explanation leaving our modern world puzzled to find a reason. The Maya calendar was constructed with astro precision impossible to understand by today's experts in the field. One of the most interesting revelations in their calculation of time is their matter-of-fact declaration that the world will end on December 23, 2012. A study of mystics, seers, psychics, and science (both Christian and non-Christian) shows that there is a kind of general agreement that the world as we know it is rushing toward destruction at break neck speed and that its movement will grind to a halt around the turn of the millennium. Even Isaac Newton, referred to earlier, seems to be among such prognosticators. While he insists that he makes no predictions *per se*, his comments about the "little horn" of Daniel and the general time for the initiation of his rule suggests that the end will fall somewhere between 2000 and 2050 A.D.

Jesus, in answering the questions of the disciples about His return, focused on a number of events which will come to pass before the consummation of the age (Matthew 24, Mark 13, Luke 21). Without hesitation, however, He warned ". . . of that day and hour knoweth no man, no, not the angels of heaven, but my Father only", (Matthew 24:36). From this statement it is learned that specific date setting is an exercise in futility, a truth verified time and again throughout the history of the church. At the same time, our Lord said, "This generation shall not pass, till all these things be fulfilled" (Matthew 24:34). What this means is that we cannot set dates but we can and should be astute enough to recognize the tenor of the times as we approach the coming day of judgment.

The "generation" is that one which will witness the ominous events foreshadowing the wrapping up of world history. Even though the particular events of which Jesus speaks will take place during the tribulation following the evacuation of the church, the rapid move in that direction will be in evidence much earlier. Let us, then, be alert to world affairs under the sway of Satanic control and not be caught like the foolish virgins unprepared to enter the wedding feast with the Bridegroom.

There is an interesting passage in the second letter to the Thessalonians (2:1-12) which appears to be misunderstood because of an unclear rendering of the King James translation and most other modern versions as well. Paul is seeking to clear up some confusion among believers who feared that they had missed the translation of the church because of the harsh persecution which they were confronting. They were wondering whether they were already in the great tribulation or, what is called "the day of the Lord", that is, the time of final judgment. In verse one he says, "Now we beseech you, brethren, by the coming of our Lord Jesus Christ, and by our gathering  together unto him . . .", a pointed reference to the coming of Christ for His church and our being caught up to be with him (see 1 Thessalonians 4:13-18). Then, in the next verse, he insists that the day of the Lord (the great tribulation) has not dawned because it will not happen until the church is evacuated. And it is at this point where the translation is misleading. Before the tribulation (the final seven years) there must be "the falling away first" after which the Antichrist will be revealed and the tribulation will commence.

The word for "the falling away" is *apostasia* from which we get the English word *apostasy*. Due to the fact that the Bible does insist that there will be an apostasy from the faith in the end times, the translators have employed that idea here. The problem is that such is not the meaning of the Greek word as used in this passage where it is preceded by the definite article and should be translated *"the departure"*. The earlier versions of the Bible (Tyndale 1534, Coverdale 1535, Cranmer 1539, and Geneva

1560) translate the word here correctly as *departure*. In a context where the word is used about a departure from doctrine, apostasy would be an acceptable word. But in this passage, Paul is not talking about doctrine but about the coming of Christ in judgment at the end of the tribulation. And it is his argument that the tribulation and judgment cannot come until the church has first departed to be with the Lord. Christ's coming for His church is imminent and can happen at any moment.

# SYMBOLISM IN NUMBERS

While no one wishes to be considered fanciful when dealing with prophecy, a word is in order since it is clear that numbers have significant meanings throughout the history of religion. One would have to be blind not to notice the symbolic use of the number seven in the Bible particularly in the book of Revelation. The number seven, however, is not the only such concern. A brief summary of the use of numbers in the written word of God follows.

ONE is ostensibly the basic number, the starting point, the beginning. Nothing is prior to one unless it is fractured. As would be expected it stands for God, the single and absolute cause of all else. It cannot be divided without becoming less than a whole. Thus it is the indivisible unit upon which the entire system is constructed.

TWO is the number of the Son of God. The Father and the Son are one, yet the Son proceeds from the Father. The nature of Christ is both divine and human, not half and half, but fully God and fully man. When represented by candles on a worship table there is one on either side of the cross symbolizing these two natures. Although the Hebrew people worshiped only one God, they referred to Him in the plural which meant that the one God is inclusive of all possible gods and clearly left room for the manifestation of the one God in more than one way. Hence, Jesus could say, "He that hath seen Me hath seen the Father".

THREE is the number of completion within the individual. The complete Godhead is Father, Son, and Holy Spirit, which is referred to in Christian doctrine as the Trinity, three in one. Man, like God, is one, yet three; he is body, soul, and spirit. Likewise the family is one in three - man, wife, and children.

FOUR is the number of the world. The world is made of four fundamental ingredients: fire, air, earth, and water. And there are four directions called north, east, south, and west. Spring, summer, fall, and winter comprise the total number of the seasons. It is interesting to note that only one of the ten commandments refers to the earth and it is number four. In Daniel and Revelation the symbol of world power is four.

SIX is the number of Satan and wickedness. The sixth letter in Revelation speaks of the trial of the church brought about by the devil. It is the opening of the sixth seal which ushers in awful destruction for the earth during the last days of evil on earth. When the sixth vial is poured out on the earth the contents are demonic spirits. Man, whose disobedience in the garden brought disgrace and death on the human race, was created on the sixth day. Satan's most evil design was wrought at the cross when Jesus was crucified on the sixth day. And the Antichrist's number is 666, a combination of three sixes or the complete individual (the number three) which still remains nothing more than man, an incomparably evil one, but still only a man, nothing more in spite of his claims.

SEVEN is the number of perfection or divine fulness. That is, it is essentially God's number - the perfection of the number one where it all commences. The seventh day of creation was a day of rest, hence the origin of the Sabbath and the sabbatical system of the Old Testament. God is portrayed in His creating glory in the Old Testament with seven spirits before the throne, the seven being symbolic of the fulness and completeness of the nature of Jehovah. This is why the seven-fold candlestick is still used in Judaism and Christianity today. It might be said that, as 666 is the number of the Antichrist, so 777 is the number of God. Daniel sees the future of Israel unfolding in a sequence of sevens. And John envisions, in the book of Revelation, seven churches embracing the Christian church worldwide from the day of Pentecost until the end of the age. There is reason to believe that Paul wrote letters to only seven churches as well, although there were scores of such established congregations of believers to which he might have addressed himself. Almost like a haunting refrain the prophet's chorus in the closing book of the Bible speaks of seven lampstands, stars, seals, trumpets, vials, beastly heads, crowns, hills, *ad infinitum.*

EIGHT is the number of new beginnings. Hebrew sons were circumcised on the eighth day. Noah was the eighth world figure and responsible for a fresh beginning after the flood. David was the eighth son of Jesse and credited with a new day for the nation of Israel. It was the eighth year designated by God for replanting the fields after the Sabbath year of rest. When John identifies the Antichrist, he sees him as the new Caesar of the restored Roman Empire, the seventh empire since Egypt, and refers to him as the eighth, a part of the seventh. That is, the Antichrist of the end time will be the representative of a world government with a new beginning. Easter was on the first day of the week, the day following the Sabbath, therefore, the eighth day. And it must be remembered that the first day of every week is the eighth.

TWELVE is the number of ultimately final, irrevocable, unalterable consummation. There are twelve hours in the day and twelve hours in the night. There are twelve months in the year. Israel was comprised of twelve tribes and the 144,000 Hebrews sealed by God during the coming tribulation is simply an amplification of the number twelve squared and raised to the thousandth degree. In the New Testament record Jesus gathered twelve men to be His disciples. These twelve became the nucleus of the Christian Church and they are not to be seen as a replacement of the tribes. The Church is not the new Israel, as it is sometimes claimed, but the Bride of Christ, whose responsibility is to be productive in bringing all men to new birth in Christ. Israel was and still is the Wife of God, unfaithful and adulterous, but God will have her back as the book of Hosea so clearly affirms. Israel was chosen as Jehovah's wife to bring all nations into His family and under His reign. When that did not happen, God chose a specific person to produce His Son, who would open the door to the Father for both Jews and Gentile. When the church day is over, Jehovah will regather His chastised people, the unfaithful Wife, to do through the Remnant what the nation at large failed to achieve.  And to return to the number twelve, there will be twelve gates to the New Jerusalem and twelve fruits from the tree of life in heaven for the healings of the nations.

Symbolic meanings may be found for other numerals and their compounds, but consideration has been given to a few of the more obvious examples.  Whatever value and importance one wishes to give to biblical or prophetic numbers is ultimately up to the student of the Word.  Some find nothing of significance in such a study, while others become obsessed with numerology.  In either case, such a position is unfortunately excessive, excessive neglect on the one hand and excessive interest on the other.  A balanced view of prophecy must, nevertheless, make room for the contribution which numbers have always made to serious inquiry.

# GREAT BALLS OF FIRE

There was a time when God saw the wickedness of man, that it was "great in the earth, and every imagination of the thoughts of his heart was only evil continually" (Genesis 6:5). That was a long time ago. But the divine diagnosis is dateless. It is descriptive of the human race from Adam's transgression in the garden of Eden to the arrogance of Antichrist at the end of the world. So we are not surprised to learn that "it repented the Lord that he had made man on the earth, and it grieved him at his heart" (Genesis 6:6). In fact, the corruption of the race was so unacceptable to the Creator that he told Noah to build an ark and warn the people that the world would be destroyed by a flood. That is history for us today, but when the warning was given it was prophecy. Every schoolchild knows the story of the flood, but not everyone is aware of the covenant made with Noah after the waters subsided. Since God knew that man would henceforth panic at the mere appearance of a thunder cloud, the Lord used the colorful arc of the rainbow as a sign that the world would never by destroyed again by water. Moses recalls the Creator's having said, "It shall come to pass, when I bring a cloud over the earth, that the bow shall be seen in the cloud; and I will remember my covenant, which is between me and you and every living creature of all flesh; and the waters shall no more become a flood to destroy all flesh. And the bow shall be in the cloud; and I will look upon it, that I may remember the everlasting covenant between God and every living creature of all flesh that is upon the earth" (Genesis 9:14-16).

A promise is a promise. And when it is made by Almighty God, we can be sure that it will be honored because He has both the power and the integrity to keep His word. But, while a world-wide flood is ruled out as an act of divine judgment, there is no suggestion that a different kind of judgment will not fall upon the human race as its corruption deepens. On the contrary, again and again the Bible confronts us with a fiery judgment far more severe than the flood of Noah. The tenor of both Old and New Testaments is that of a fiery holocaust at the end of the world. Peter describes it in graphic terms as he writes, "the day of the Lord will come as a thief in the night, in which the heavens shall pass away with a great noise, and the elements shall melt with fervent heat; the earth also, and the works that are in it, shall be burned up. Seeing, then, that all these things shall be dissolved, what manner of persons ought ye to be in all holy living and godliness, looking for and hasting unto the coming of the day of God, in which the heavens, being on fire, shall be dissolved, and the elements shall melt with fervent heat?" (2 Peter 3:10-12).

It is more than just interesting that the next instance of destructive divine judgment following the flood was not world wide but limited to a geographical area near the Dead Sea known as Sodom and Gomorrah. The reason for the wrath of God was the same as in the case of the flood, "their sin is very grievous" (Genesis 18:20). When the judgment came to Sodom it was not a flood of water but a rain of fire, a fact in keeping with the Lord's promise. Moses records the event in the following words, "The Lord rained upon Sodom and upon Gomorrah brimstone and fire from the Lord out of heaven. . . . And Abraham got up early in the morning to the place where he stood before the Lord. and he looked toward Sodom and Gomorrah, and toward all the land of the plain, and beheld, and, lo, the smoke of the country went up as the smoke of a furnace" (Genesis 19:24, 27-28). Of considerable significance is Peter's discussion of the destruction of Sodom and Gomorrah in the same prophetic discourse in which he portrays the final destruction of the world as being similar to that of Sodom (2 Peter 2:4-3:12). It is also noteworthy that in these verses the writer makes reference to the flood as a certainty that God will judge the world system again, except the next time it will be by fire.

Fire is an oft-recurring method of divine judgment in both Testaments (Genesis 19:24; Exodus 9:23; Leviticus 10; Numbers 11:1,

16:35; 2 Kings 1:10; Amos 7:4; 2 Thessalonians 1:8; Revelation 8:8). This adds to the reason for believing that the world will end in a blazing fire. And it is in keeping with what is being said by many of the leading astro-scientists of our time. Students of the skies are warning us that man could be in for a hot time of it. Great balls of fire are hurling through space at unimaginable velocity, with mammoth proportions, and cremating heat. Every moment of the day and night our earth is threatened by thousands of giant asteroids, fireballs from outer space, any one of which could obliterate the planet. Scientists insist that entire civilizations have been destroyed by giant burning masses crashing through the atmosphere into the hard crust of the earth. But the shocking reality is that it could happen again and there would be absolutely nothing we would be able to do to stop it. A sizeable part of our space program is devoted to looking for asteroids. It is possible that the fiery impact of a comet or similar object, with explosive power a million times that of the bomb which fell on Hiroshima, would kill nearly everyone on the planet if not all. To envision the scene of a world on fire -- infernos ignited one after another by the intense heat, tidal waves of enormous magnitude, volcanic eruptions like none we have ever seen, floods battling the flames and dust confronting the waves - - is beyond the fantasy of the most imaginative among us. And yet this is what Peter seems to be warning us about two thousand years prior to the growing interest and alarm of modern science.

While no one is knowledgeable enough to predict precisely what method He who is "The alpha and the omega" will employ to bring about the death of the world system and the restoration of the heavens and the earth, it appears to be a universal suspicion that fire will play a major roll. The earth is a powder keg with a short fuse and it is lighted. Man himself may finally bring about his own fiery demise. Judgment is not something God does to us, rather it is something that we bring on ourselves. Around the world the flames of revolution are raging. Man is engaged in a civil war with his own people and a growing revolution against

God. The average person from Africa to Europe to Russia to the Americas sees his world falling to pieces while he has nightmares of cataclysmic collapse all over the world. Never have so many efforts been made to bring about peace and order, but they are fruitless. Everything is on fire and there seems to be little reason to hope for any break from the heat in the kingdom of man. Some scientists argue that the universe started with a big bang. That is probably wrong. It is much more likely that it will end with one.

# RESTORATION IS NOT ANNIHILATION

When the apostle John writes about the new heavens and the new earth in the book of Revelation, he does not mean annihilation and replacement. Nothing God has created will ever be destroyed. It may change forms like a lump of coal becomes energy and cinders when burned, but the work of God described in the opening chapters of Genesis will never perish. Only the defilement of creation for which man is responsible will be destroyed. In that sense, the heavens and the earth will one day be new, changed but not exchanged.

That which will happen to the universe at the end of time will be similar to what happens to a person when he is born again. He becomes "a new creation" in Christ Jesus (2 Corinthians 5:17), the old life of sin and shame is put to death and a new life commences. Old things are done away, everything is new. No one takes this to mean that the person is annihilated and replaced by another. It is evident that there has been no department store kind of exchange, one item for another, but that the man or woman made new in Christ is cleaned up and marvelously changed. This is expressed especially well by the oft-used description of salvation as a new birth. Equally descriptive of individual salvation and the changes in the heavens and the earth at the end of the world is the term conversion.

An illustration is helpful here. In my garage is parked a beautiful little car which has been my pride for many years. It is a 1968 Volkswagen Beetle with too many miles on it to count. When the little fellow came into my hands it was already twenty years old and it had been mistreated and abused to the point of being hardly more than rusty junk. But nobody can believe his eyes when he sees it now. At considerable expense and over too many hours to admit from the present owner, the old rusty car has been made new! Parts have been removed and others added, corroded areas have been cared for, mechanical malfunctions corrected, worn upholstery and door panels reconditioned. And a gorgeous raspberry red paint has brought the little bug back to life. It is made new, not replaced but rebuilt from scratch. The whole procedure which has just been explained is commonly called restoration. And that is what John is envisioning in the last book of the Bible when he sees a new heaven and a new earth. My Volkswagen is still the same car as it was in 1968 when a group of German automakers put it together, but it is gloriously new, even more beautiful than when it rolled off the showroom floor. Several years ago, while having our family car serviced at the local dealer from which we had purchased it, my feet just naturally carried me into the new car exhibition area. And there, as I caught my breath, sat a gleaming white 1955 Ford Thunderbird which had been restored to immaculate perfection and was tempting someone to buy it and take it home. It was not a new car, and yet it was! As my unwilling feet took me back to the service area to get our readied car, it occurred to me that the vision of loveliness which still haunts me was a 1993/1955 Thunderbird. And so it will be for believing Christians on the resurrection morning when man and his world will be new.

One further comparison. One evening on a television interview, a well-known star of the screen who had been involved in a recent accident which left him a paraplegic, in answer to a question, made the following statement. Man is not his body, explained the immobilized man, he is a spirit and soul. Although it is impossible to know the depths of his brave words, the statement itself was faultlessly accurate. Our bodies are houses in which we live, necessary habitats for living in a material world. For most of us either disease or time, perhaps an accident, will render the body frail and inadequate for continuing the unhampered life to which we once were accustomed. Our old houses are getting shaky. Eventually they will be condemned and we will not be permitted to live in them anymore. It will appear that they have been torn down, but actually our bodies will be under renovation, a kind of divine recycling.

Sometimes storms, floods, fire, and the wear and tear of the elements in general reduce the mortgaged dwellings in which we live with our families to uninhabitable domicile. Frankly, the situation often gets so desperate that either the insurance company or plain common sense dictates that we move out for a while until the needed corrections are made. During that time a motel may become a welcome paradise where we wait for the carpenters, plumbers, and electricians to restore the old place to its original lustre. Then the welcome news is broken to us and we move back in with amazement at the change. No question about it, the house is the same one we moved away from but splendidly different. So different, in fact, that the whole family would swear the edifice to be a new house if they did not watch the entire work project as it progressed. "Behold," declares the Lord, "I make all things new" (Revelation 21:5).

When Jesus sought to assure His disciples about the future, He said, "I go to prepare a place for you" (John 14:2). This is not to be thought of as some different planet or star to which God will one day take us when the task is finished. The place being prepared is the new heavens and the new earth, even the "new Jerusalem coming down from God out of heaven prepared as a bride adorned for her husband" (Revelation 21:2). Behind the scenes being played out on the stage of human events, the Creating Father and His angels are preparing this world for the day when the fires of refining judgment will torch the system of world government with all its attendant ego-centered contaminants. And when the smoke clears away, that which remains will be the new heavens and the new earth. Like gold tried in the fire, our bodies and our world will be returned to God's people pure and clean. During the great tribulation the Father will put the final touches on His renovation program while believers are away in Paradise awaiting the moment when we will move back to a totally restored world. In the meantime let none of us forget that "God is not slack concerning His promise" (2 Peter 3:9).

# WHAT TO EXPECT WHEN CHRISTIANS LEAVE THIS WORLD

When the discipline of prophecy is undertaken it is because the seeker after truth is more than a little concerned with what the future holds in store for the human race. That includes an interest in whether the world is going to end and, if it is, how it will happen. It also includes what is to follow, if anything, the collapse of civilization as we know it. There is little to be gained by pulling the covers over one's head and pretending that nothing is going to happen. The second law of thermo-dynamics insists that everything is wearing out. And that means that time must have a stop. Certainly, if Christ tarries His coming we are all going to die and every sane thinking person is keenly interested in that. For this reason we will do well to consider the Christians' death, what it means and where it leads.

In the event the Lord does not return for His church in our lifetime, what will happen to the believer at the moment of death? The one thing which will not happen is the end of life. The body will cease to function to be sure, but life is more than the body which is only a tent in which the Christian dwells until he no longer needs it. According to the two accounts of creation in Genesis, God created man in the image and likeness of the Creator Himself. None of the animals earlier mentioned in the first account were fashioned in similar manner. God is a Spirit and the body of man has nothing to do with divine likeness. Therefore, man was made a spiritual being first and was subsequently given a body and soul as recorded in the second account (see Genesis 1:26-27; 2:7). When the body fails at death, the true being of man is unaffected since he has forfeited nothing but his house which was only lent to him for living in a corporeal and material world. The spirit returns unto the God from whom it came. So death is not the end of life. Life goes on in a different dimension.

The traditional explanation of the difference between man and the lower animal kingdom is that Adam was created as a body first, then God "breathed into his nostrils the breath of life and man became a living soul". The word *soul* in the Hebrew Old Testament is the same as that earlier translated "living creature" by the Authorized Version. This would mean, then, that all animal life is possessed of *soul* which fundamentally suggests the living, moving, breathing, animated essence of both man and beast. It is not the *soul* which distinguishes man from everything else, but the spirit. That is his kinship with the Creator. It is that which gives him his eternal quality. So man is essentially a spiritual being with a body and soul, not a body with a spirit. The two accounts of creation, the second a more detailed description of the first, make this crystal clear.

Jesus provides us with insight into this whole matter when He breaks the encrusted traditions from the mind of Nicodemus by pointing out that, in order to get to heaven, a man must "be born of water and the Spirit" (John 3:15). Here the Lord is contrasting natural birth (by water) and the second birth (by the Spirit). It is the spirit of man reborn by the Spirit of God which makes one like the Creator and, therefore, entitled to live forever. The likeness of God, given to Adam at creation, was defaced by the fall into disobedience. As a result, man began to die, the body suffering the consequences of the death blow to the spirit. The whole race, then, is marked by this debilitating proneness because we are all "dead in trespasses and sins". But the new birth fans the sparks of our dying spirits into an open flame and life eternal.

Luke records a teaching lesson given by Jesus in the sixteenth chapter of his gospel narrative which opens many windows on the state of men and women after death. There is no reason to consider these words as a parable since the Lord gives a personal name to one of the characters, something He never does anywhere else in a parabolic story. The two persons in the lesson, Lazarus and the rich man, both die and their bodies are buried.

But neither of them ceases to be. Life goes on after the tents in which they lived have been consigned to the grave. Lazarus is literally "carried by the angels into Abraham's bosom", an expression of the Jewish Talmud for the state of bliss after death. But the rich man finds himself in *hades* (not *hell* as the authorized version mistranslates the word) where he is "in torment" and begs for Lazarus to be given permission to bring water to cool his tongue from the flames. Discovering that such a request cannot be granted (there will be no change in eternal destiny for anyone after death), the rich man makes a second attempt to somehow get word to his brothers lest they also miss the bliss of Abraham's bosom.

One of the inescapable lessons learned from this provocative story told by our Lord is in verse twenty-six, "Between us and you there is a great gulf fixed, so that they who would pass from here to you cannot; neither can they pass to us, that would come from there". In addition to the fact that these words suggest that death fixes our eternal destination, they also assure us that the spirits of the departed are in one of two very different places and that there is a no-man's land or boundary between them. It should also be observed that in both places, Abraham's bosom where Lazarus is said to have been and hades where the rich man was, there is no "soul sleep", as some insist, but complete consciousness. The dead are alive and conscious without the body or tent which is an inanimate state until the resurrection. These two places in the other world are referred to in the Old Testament as *sheol* and in the New Testament as *hades*, both words meaning the same thing, one Hebrew and the other Greek. Although both these words are sometimes translated "grave", they never suggest a place of burial, but the state of the spirit following death. What then is the significance of the foregoing observation? It is simply that Jesus accepted and amplified the general belief of the Hebrew community that the wicked and the righteous lived on after death in separate wings of a place called *hades*. Had our Lord known this concept to be wrong He would have employed a different lesson which would have corrected the current error while still imparting the central truth emphasized by the story.

When Christ was dying on the cross the two thieves dying on either side of him engaged in an agonizing conversation about who this central figure might really be. One taunted Jesus with jeers and mockery while the other, aware of his own crimes and conscious of the innocence of Christ, acknowledged his sin and asked to be remembered when the Lord entered his kingdom. Jesus reply was, "Today shalt thou be with me in paradise" which Paul later referred to as "the third heaven". And John in Revelation (2:7) mentions paradise as having to do with the "tree of life" where God dwells. There is little question but that the apostle John thinks of paradise as the restoration of the Garden of Eden where the tree of life is first seen. Life after death, according to the beloved disciple, is what John Milton called "Paradise Regained". And there can be no debate about the word as used by Jesus. Paradise was where He was going. And it was where the believing thief would be with Him.

Saturday of Holy Week was moving day for the Old Testament saints in *hades*, the wing earlier defined as Abraham's bosom. The righteous ones, children of Abraham by faith in Jesus Christ, were waiting for the day of their deliverance when the final sacrifice for sin would be paid by the Messiah. While His body lay in the tomb on Saturday, He who had been accused of laboring on the Sabbath, was busier than ever as He descended into *hades* to empty the saved wing of that place and take the saints with Him into paradise. This is what Paul is thinking about in Ephesians where he quotes the Psalmist (68:18), "When he ascended up on high, he led captivity captive, and gave gifts unto men". Then the apostle explains, "Now that he ascended, what is it but that he also descended first into the lower parts of the earth?" (Ephesians 4:8-9). Peter seems to make reference to this wondrous truth when he declares, "For Christ also hath once suffered for sins, the just for the unjust, that he might bring us to God, being put to death in the flesh but made alive by the Spirit, by whom also he went and preached unto the spirits in prison, who at one time were disobedient, when once the long suffering of God waited in the days of Noah, while the ark was preparing . . ." (1 Peter 3:18-20). To be sure, Peter speaks only of the proclamation made in *hades* to the pre-flood wicked (the final irrevocable verdict that the sentence would be carried out to the fullest extent of divine justice), but logic alone would insist that, by the same token, the judge of all the earth would have announced to the believing saints that the day of their deliverance had also come.

What happens to the dead who die in the Lord? This was the question which sparked this lengthy discourse on life after death. Prior to the death of Christ on the cross, the righteous remained in Abraham's bosom awaiting the solution for sin for which the sacrificial system of the Old Testament was but a temporary arrangement. But, since the death of Christ, every believer goes immediately into the presence of the Lord which is called paradise. And where is that? No one knows although it is probably another dimension of the Creator's universal domain. Wherever it is, one thing is sure, Christ is there and that is enough to make any place a paradise.

The unbeliever still waits on death row (hades) in a kind of holding room for the final judgment. The believer, however, is with the Lord, and since Christ is with His church unto the ends of the age, He cannot be far away. If that is so, then our loved ones are near to us, much like the "great cloud of witnesses" (Hebrews 12:1) whose encouragement moves us to continuing faithfulness. Quite a distinction was given to the confessing thief on the cross. He was the first person to miss the trip to hades. He did not have to wait for a solution to his sin problem. The solution was hanging on a cross by his side.

No more appropriate way could be found for bringing to a conclusion these additional notes on our study of biblical prophecy. Inevitably, some will question the need for such study. Therefore, it must be pointed out that there are two reasons for any intensive investigation into this largely untapped mine. First, prophecy must not be neglected because it is a confirmation of God's Word when it comes to pass. Second, the masses must be warned of the awful consequences of unbelief and such cannot be done without specific reference to what the Bible has to say about the future. These concluding paragraphs, however, help us to understand that the hope of the world is Jesus Christ. Whether we are caught up to be with the Lord at His promised return or die before that long-awaited day arrives, the result is the same. The Christian - the real, believing, and obedient Christian - is soon going to be with his redeeming Lord of lords and King of kings. This is our hope. This is our strength. This is our joy.

# WHAT THEN SHALL WE DO?

Jesus Christ is inescapable. That He is the most disturbing character in the annals of history is beyond dispute. When Pilate asked the elders of Israel, "What then shall I do with Jesus who is called Christ?" (Matthew 27:22), he was confronted with the absolute impossibility of detouring around the prisoner before him. Neither could the elders, to whom he put the question, evade their own confrontation. While the nations leaders wanted Pontius Pilate to face up to his responsibility as governor, there was no way they could avoid being accountable as well.

Men can look into the eyes of Jesus and reject him. We are free to decide either for him or against him. But no one is free to ignore him. And the day comes eventually to all of us when the question is no longer, "What shall I do with Jesus?" but "What will He do with me?" When He comes back to earth, it will be in judgment. And what Jesus does with us then will be determined by what we do with him now.

The study of prophecy is never an end in itself. On the contrary, such a study is an indispensable tool of evangelism which alerts us to the inevitability of judgment day. Regrettably, some will always be caught up in Biblical prophecy as an intellectual pursuit alone. But God did not leave us this detailed chart of the future in order that we might massage the minds of the public with our clairvoyant talents.

Twenty-five percent of the entire Bible is devoted to prophecy because it is his divine will that no one should be in the dark about the end of history. Neither does He desire that we ignore the direction which the world is taking as we approach that end. So large a portion of scripture would suggest that God is telling us something of eternal significance, something which can be ignored only at one's own peril.

To summarize a few of the signs of the season at which time Christ will come again, the following should be noted.

1. The rebirth of the nation of Israel is the most important sign of all. Not since 70 A.D. had the Jewish people enjoyed a land of their own until 1948. The return of Abraham's descendants to their homeland was predicted in the Bible as a clear sign of the second coming of Jesus (Luke 21:24).

2. As we near the end the moral atmosphere of the world will be at an all-time low. Since the middle of the twentieth century we have been witness to a shocking spiral downward in morality (2 Timothy 3:1-4).

3. Could there be any more visible proof of the return of Christ than the unsettled state of the entire world? With the alarming increase in violence and tribal conflict, as well as the starving multitudes, we remember the warning of Jesus himself (Matthew 24:6-8).

4. The frightening increase in terrestrial upheavals is foretold in the book which has never been wrong. Of earthquakes registering 6.0 or above, fifty-one occurred from 1940 to 1950. Each decade thereafter reveals an astounding escalation in their number, 1990 to 2000 producing 1,514 such quakes (Matthew 24:7).

5. A profound increase in knowledge cannot be overlooked. With the aid of computers, the youngest children among us have accumulated factual knowledge beyond that which anyone imagined a few short years ago (Daniel 12:4).

6. The direction of government and religion is moving at breakneck speed toward one world. The New World Order of the coming Antichrist and the New Age philosophy embracing pagan and cultic beliefs, with Christianity reduced to an indistinguishable piece of the vast amalgam, is a sign which cannot be missed (Matthew 24:15, 24).

These are only a few of the scores of signs relating to the return of Christ showing up everywhere. Even the most unconcerned person cannot fail to notice them. These signs are the hope of the redeemed and, at the same time, the judgment of the world. However, there is no credible reason why anyone has to be unprepared for the great and terrible day of the Lord.

Having said this, one thing remains to be done in order to insure our lives against the ultimate disaster. The impending doom faced by the Philippian jailer (Acts 16:25-34) was nothing compared to that awaiting the man or woman who is unprepared for the return of Christ. The question which the frightened jailer asked, however, was the correct one, both for himself and for the rest of us. And what was that question? "What must I do to be saved?" Multitudes of people in our churches do not really know what they must do to be saved. And lest none of us overlook the urgency, the word must leaves no doubt that taking a chance on salvation is sure destruction.

Nicodemus was a genuinely religious man when he came to Jesus with the haunting suspicion that something was lacking in his life. With all his religious observances, there was an unsettling awareness that the whole point had been sadly missed. He fasted, prayed, gave alms, observed the traditions, and taught at the seminary. Jesus stunned this deeply religious man with the fact that all such efforts at being accepted by God were only skin-deep and never touched the dormant spirit.

Nicodemus' problem was that he was trying to act alive when he was really dead, "dead in trespasses and sins" (Ephesians 2:1). The only solution to his inner problem lay in starting over again. "Don't be surprised," said Jesus, "you must be born again" (John 3:7). Nicodemus responded as we all might, "How can these things be?"

Well, how can they? How does a man go about being born the second time? The first thing is to acknowledge that our self-centeredness is destroying us, that there is an image in our hearts of what ought to be, but it is being continually marred by sin. Herein lies the basic hang-up. Nobody wants to admit to sin anymore. One may confess to being neurotic or even psychotic, but nobody will acknowledge that he is a sinner. Until we do, there is no possibility of advancing to step two.

Once we have confessed our sinfulness, we are ready to ask for God's forgiveness. Ours is a merciful God, full of compassion and love. Remember his promise: "If we confess our sins, he is faithful and just to forgive us our sins and to cleanse us from all unrighteousness" (1 John 1:9). The incredibly amazing thing about divine forgiveness is that it is available for the asking. Of course, that is what grace is all about – it is a free gift.

In the third place, the penitent sinner, who has repented with confession and asked for forgiveness, must believe that God hears him and will do exactly as He has promised. "He who comes to God must believe that he is and that he is a rewarder of those who diligently seek him" (1 John 1:9). When Paul says, "Believe on the Lord Jesus Christ and thou shalt be saved" (Acts 16:31), he is actually promising that, if we put our full weight on Jesus, He will never let us down. Trust him! Rely on him! You can count on Jesus Christ. And that is right. When Jesus had the chance to save himself from the cross, He thought of us and stretched out his arms and died, died for our sins. The Son of God went to that cross to pay a debt He did not owe for us who owe a debt we cannot pay. One can depend on that when everything else fails.

The last step is discipleship, walking with Jesus and learning at his feet. And when a believer sits there, he will hear our Lord say, "Whoever desires to come after me, let him deny himself, and take up his cross, and follow me" (Mark 8:34). Being a Christian carries with it the recognition of a higher goal. In obedience, the new-born child of God must become a partner with Christ, bearing some of the weight of the cross, devoting his life to the redemptive work of leading others to know the Lord.

It all sounds so simple, but the rewards are so great. In boundless love, God made sure that man could be redeemed without a complex and difficult procedure of rites and regulations. The cross is the divine initiative by which God reconstructs, out of a broken relationship, the joy of reconciliation. We have only to accept that overture of divine love.

In view of the ominous future which the word of God makes clear, it behooves us to accept the only way of salvation known to a lost world. Knowing that some person who reads this book needs to get ready for Christ's return to earth, the following prayer is suggested.

Dear God, I believe that you sent
Jesus Christ, your only Son, to die on the
cross for my sin that I may have eternal
life. Today I acknowledge my sins and accept
Christ as my Savior and Lord. Come into
my heart, Lord Jesus. Amen